FLUTIE!

by
Ian Thomsen

The
Globe
Pequot
Press

Chester, Connecticut 06412

Library of Congress Catalog Card Number 84-63145

ISBN: 0-87106-881-8

Manufactured in the United States of America
First printing January 1985

Contents

*To Mom, Dad
and Glenn*

Acknowledgements

First I must thank my *Boston Globe* colleague, Will McDonough. This book was his idea.

Thanks also to:

Vince Doria, the *Globe* sports editor and, for one day in December, 1984, my personal copyeditor.

Don Skwar, who helped tighten things up and looked for pictures.

Bill Brett, who orchestrated the photos' duplication by James Bulman and John Ioven.

Linda Kennedy, Kevin Lynch and Kate Bandos of Globe Pequot Press, who dropped everything to do it right.

Charles Everitt, president of Globe Pequot, who kept me aware of deadlines, encouraged me and is basically responsible for this.

The Boston Globe sportswriters, whose Boston College and Flutie articles of the last several years proved invaluable.

Tim Everitt, for rushing the final proofs to the printer.

Sheraton Hotel's room service, for getting me through that long night in Seattle.

And Purolator. Everything arrived on time.

1

Introduction

When I joined *The Boston Globe* in July 1983, I was told again and again how much I would enjoy covering Boston College football. "That Flutie," people would say. "He's really exciting." So I looked at Flutie's statistics. In 1982, his sophomore year, he had thrown 20 interceptions and 13 touchdowns. Not very impressive.

The first rule I learned was not to trust statistics. Doug Flutie ran circles around them. The numbers were an indication of his general improvement as a quarterback, but had little to do with the outcome of games. Those afternoons he completed, say, only 15 of 40 passes—and there were a few days like those—he probably made up for it by running for 80 yards, and BC probably won. In Doug Flutie's last three years as a player, BC lost only six regular season games.

One peculiarity, noticed while watching his junior season and from reading accounts of the previous two years, was that his most exciting games were those he *lost* to the powerful teams: Pittsburgh in 1981, Penn State in '82 and '84, West Virginia in '83. By the second half, the essence of those games had become the opponents' players and coaches and support systems all trying to stop little Doug Flutie. Though BC would lose, there would be so many great plays, so many times when he could have won. He deserved to win. My strongest memory was that of seeing him, on the TV monitor in the press box, standing alone on the sideline after throwing his third interception late in the 27-17 loss to West Virginia in '83. *Doug vs. World. World wins, but it was close.* Flutie was at his best when he was most vulnerable. Like Bobby Layne, he never lost. He just ran out of time.

After games, he could discuss in detail every play. He was cooperative, sometimes more so after losses. It appeared he had to talk about them, what had gone wrong, so he could get onto the business of winning next week. But after victories, especially the big ones of his senior year, he seemed almost depressed. While his teammates were celebrating the comeback win at Alabama, Flutie was surrounded by reporters on deadline.

The attention finally beat him down. After he had returned to school from his nine grueling days of Heisman appearances in December 1984, I waited for him in Alumni Stadium while he ran wind sprints with teammates. I had been assigned to ask him and other players how they planned to spend Christmas. "I guess I'll be home," Flutie said while he played catch with his brother and teammate, Darren.

Well, I said, at least it will be a day of privacy for you.

"Hopefully," Doug said. He was bitter. "Unless somebody stops by the house."

No one would do that on Christmas.

"It's been known to happen," he said. "I wouldn't put it past 'em."

Of course, by the time I was done talking with other players, Doug was laughing, playing 2-on-1 football with Darren and a roommate.

Flutie was like his coach, Jack Bicknell, in a lot of ways. "We have a unique relationship," Bicknell said.

"We don't talk a lot. When we have something to discuss, he comes in, and we talk about it, and then he leaves." By Flutie's senior year, they were talking similarly. Flutie would laugh in the middle of a sentence the way his coach would, or tell a story the way Bicknell did, exaggerating how he felt before an event to build the event itself into a better story. Doug lacked Bicknell's sense of humor, but his charisma made up for that.

Other tactical similarities between coach and player were more significant. Most important was that both liked throwing the ball. They didn't like conservative games. It was a backward offense, passing the ball to set up the running game. Most teams did it the other way around.

Bicknell and his assistants can take much credit for Flutie's improvement. But he also improved every year because he wanted to and because he had to—the offense was predicated on what Flutie could do at his best. When he proved he could stay in the pocket, read defenses and avoid interceptions, defenses then had to concentrate on stopping a sound, standard Boston College passing offense. And that made Flutie's scrambles all the more dangerous—at any time he was capable of doing something that could totally surprise the defense.

After he had grasped the fundamentals, there is no doubt that he was the best quarterback in the nation his senior year. He took the next step. He came back and BC beat Alabama. And then he threw That Pass in Miami. Flutie 2, World 0. Given another year, would the next step have been a national championship? We'll never know, because if there's one thing we learned from all of this, it's that when time runs out, the game's over.

2

Foundation

The interview to become head coach at a big-time football school—well, at a school that played a big-time football schedule—had gone well. So well that the next day, Jack Bicknell and his golf clubs were on a plane to Florida. While Boston College was deciding whom to hire for the 1981 football season, Bicknell was planning to attend a coaches' convention in Miami and play golf. "I'd felt good about interviews many times before," he explained, "and nothing had come of it."

The way he figured it, the world came down to figuring how to make a living, and then living it like heck. Jack Bicknell's life wasn't a money-making proposition but money never did get him going in the morning. Cowboy boots carried him into the office and country-and-western rhythms kept the toes tapping. The lyrics? He lived them.

He had played four sports at North Plainfield High School, N.J., but he rode a football scholarship to Rutgers. One day he broke his neck badly enough to keep him from playing football again. So he came home, played three sports at Montclair State, and coached football as a volunteer at North Plainfield High School. Ten years later Bicknell was head coach of the New Jersey state champion, Governor Livingston High School. Meanwhile, his first quarterback at North

Plainfield, Pete Carmichael, had joined the newly-forming coaching staff at Boston College. He recommended that Bicknell be hired to coach offensive backs, and BC head coach Joe Yukica interviewed Bicknell for 15 minutes in a New York airport. Sold.

So in 1968, Jack Bicknell became an assistant coach at Boston College.

His BC backfield outscored opponents 270-27 in the final half of 1974, but by then he was looking to be a *college* head coach. Colgate, Union, and Middlebury said no before the University of Maine hired him in 1976, and Jack rubbed his hands and brought his wife Lois and the kids to Orono. "A great place to bring up a family," he said. Maine gave him $4,346 for grants-in-aid that year. Other schools in the Yankee Conference were allowed 65 scholarships. No problem. "I always just figured it could be done," he said.

But how to do it? He would walk the campus, searching for someone to play for him. He looked for every edge he could imagine. One day his search led him to the drawer in his desk, and the NCAA football rule book. Rule 9, Section 4, Article 1: A batted backward pass becomes a free ball.

In 1978, with 23 seconds left in the first quarter at New Hampshire, Bicknell called the play. "Bat Ball," he said. His assistant coaches shook their heads and walked away. His players giggled. Across the field, Bicknell stared at his friend, New Hampshire coach Bill Bowes. "I didn't want to do it against him," Bicknell said, "because I didn't want to embarrass him. But we're in the mud at New Hampshire, and we've got to try something, and it's right there in the rule book."

Maine assumed field goal position from the New Hampshire 28. The ball was snapped to holder Tony Trafton. He tossed it to kicker Mike Hodgson. Hodgson volleyball-punched it into the end zone. Tight end Dave Higgins fell on it. Touchdown, Maine.

Teams everywhere tried the play that season. "People even started doing it against us," Bicknell said. His national reputation had begun. Emory Bellard invented the wishbone offense. Bill Yeoman had the veer. And the Bat Ball was Jack Bicknell's, until the NCAA outlawed it after the season.

*   *   *

So that was his story. Now, if he could make it rhyme, he could play it on his guitar, even sing it, when no one was listening. "I love country," he said. "I don't know why. The words. I love the words. Building the railroads and prisons and things like that."

One day, *Boston Globe* sportswriter Bob Duffy would nickname him Cowboy Jack. It would be the supreme compliment, especially since Bicknell had never lived south of New Jersey.

Enough reminiscing. The plane was landing in Miami, and soon he was walking out of the airport, heading for the Fontainebleau Hotel. He liked the clinics at these conventions, listening to the ideas someone had used against the Penn States and Alabamas. On this afternoon, Jack Bicknell was 42 years old, and he was a head college football coach.

That night he called up to Orono to check on the family.

Lois was crying.

"My gosh," Bicknell thought, "one of the kids must be sick."

"Mr. Flynn just phoned," Lois said. "You're the new Boston College coach."

Impossible. Sure, he had interviewed, but that had been the goal in itself. The note he'd written to Bill Flynn, the BC athletic director, had said he would like to talk about the job. "If you feel you could grant me an interview, I would appreciate it," the letter read. "But if not, I understand."

Now here he was, flying standby to Boston, rushing off and leaving the golf clubs and phone calls to his convention roommate, Bill Bowes. Head coach of the Boston College Eagles? The song kept getting better.

But he was heading into some rough country. In Boston, the alumni drew before the new coach could find his holster. In the hours preceding his inaugural press conference, Bicknell awoke to the *Boston Herald*. "Snub of Gallup angers some 'Bald Eagles,' " announced the headline.

The Bald Eagles were alumni who had witnessed BC's last period of football greatness, which had coincided with the last world war. Coach Frank Leahy had arrived at Boston College in 1939, declaring, "I did not come to BC to fail." Nor did he stay for long. He took the Eagles to their first two bowl games, winning a national championship at the 1941 Sugar Bowl, and then, 11 days after signing a 5-year contract, he left for Notre Dame. The Eagles played in the 1943 Orange Bowl without him. That was all. BC's bowl history filled one page in the media guide, with the help of a very large photo.

The alums' remembrances of bowls past during the following 38 years probably won a few fans to their side, and bored the rest of Boston against them. With an opening-season victory, the Bald Eagles would immediately begin talking about a fourth bowl game . . . with three wins came squawking dreams of a national championship. Then the Eagles invariably would lose to Villanova, and the rest of Boston had the final laugh.

The worst atrocity to the Leahy memory was BC's 0-11 season in 1978. Though coach Ed Chlebek recovered to finish 7-4 in 1980, the pressure was too much. BC had scheduled him against Top 10 teams while allowing him only six assistants; other schools had eight. His stadium seated only 32,000. His desk had been dropped into a dark, shabby little hole called the Head Coach's Office, which was across the hall from a dark, shabby bigger hole called the Weight Room. One day he asked for an extension of his contract and was turned down. He resigned, accepting an easier job at Kent State.

The apparent successor was 34-year-old Barry Gallup, a handsome assistant coach who unabashedly announced his love for Boston College. "Coaching is all I've ever wanted to do and BC is the only place I've ever wanted to be," he said. His middle names was Charles, so he could have been known as B.C. Gallup, but there he drew the line. Call him Barry, he would say, shaking hands, laughing, recalling names of 2,000 acquaintances ago. One afternoon while he was setting BC receiving records in 1968-69, he dived to catch a touchdown pass and slid out of the end zone. On his back, he looked up at *Boston Globe* photographer Frank O'Brien. "Did you get it?" Gallup asked.

He turned down an offer to play for the NFL's New England Patriots, and became instead a BC assistant coach upon graduation in 1969. Following the 0-11 of 1978, Navy coach George Welsh asked Gallup to join his staff, which had returned from a bowl game. No thank you, Gallup said. Wake Forest offered him an assistant's job worth a $5,000 raise in 1980. Gallup talked to Flynn, the AD, about that one. "He felt very highly about loyalty and said that my time would come," Gallup said.

So when Chlebek left, every BC coach recommended that Flynn hire Barry Gallup. Several alumni backed him. Before Bicknell had even been interviewed, he had read on the front page that BC would hire Gallup. The phone didn't seem to stop ringing with friends asking that Gallup consider hiring them as assistants.

Until January 7, 1981. The day Lois Bicknell broke down in happiness.

The Bald Eagles could not wait for Bicknell's plane to land.

"My reaction is disappointment," said Dr. Tom Giblin, whose father had been the dentist for BC's Sugar Bowl team. "We should have promoted a man like Barry Gallup from within the ranks. Lack of head coaching experience doesn't disqualify the man. I can think of two other successful coaches who got their head coaching breaks while they were still assistant coaches. Joe Paterno has done all right at Penn State, and Frank Leahy . . ."

"His record even at the level that Maine plays at is not impressive," said Paul Brooks, who attended BC in the mid-1950s. "I think all this says something about the program. No successful head coach in a major college applied for the job."

And now, the final blow from the alumnus "who wished to remain anonymous," but had been described by friends as a "keen observer with substantial clout":

"Bicknell's selection was an extremely bad appointment. Boston College had Bicknell as an assistant for five or six years. He was never an outstanding coach. He was well known there as the last man to arrive for practices and the first off the field at night. He was a pleasant, personable man of good character, but just not a first-class football coach. And he had an extremely poor record in Maine, regardless of any excuses about no scholarships, level of play, whatever."

On January, 7, 1981, Boston College officially announced that Jack Bicknell was its 29th football coach.

"What's the worst thing that could happen to me?" he would say. "I could get fired. I might get hit with a tomato from the stands. So what?"

*   *   *

Barry Gallup soon agreed to remain as Bicknell's recruiting coordinator and receivers coach. With the exception of quarterback coach Tom Coughlin, hired from Syracuse, and Pete Carmichael, the other assistants assigned to lead the Eagles out of the days of war bonds had no major college coaching experience. Most had come with Bicknell from Maine.

He could either sit back and fret that recruiting season was at least a month old, or he could go out and recruit like heck. Bicknell needed to find a quarterback. He had been hired because of his offensive style: He liked to throw 22 to 25 times per game. "I believe in a quarterback-oriented offense," he said the night he was hired. "You do what your quarterback can do."

Gallup had found *the* quarterback, and he could do everything. Run. Throw (55 percent completions for 3,421 yards and 15 touchdowns). Win (his high school team was 38-1). His name? Peter Muldoon.

Long before Ed Chlebek's resignation, Peter Muldoon had been Gallup's No. 1 project. Gallup had recruited and signed Peter's brother Casey in 1977. He stayed at the Muldoon home during recruiting trips to Washington, D.C., before Peter had become a prospect. Gallup was planning to bring the national letter of intent to Muldoon's home when Peter called and asked for another week to decide. One problem was Holy Cross and its new coach, Rick Carter. Another was Holy Cross alumnus, Baltimore Orioles owner and trial lawyer Edward Bennett Williams, an influential man. He talked, he lectured, he discussed the situation with Muldoon. Worcester never looked better. Neither did Holy Cross, because in the winter of 1981, it had Peter Muldoon's signature on a scholarship form.

A crushing loss, but Gallup hadn't run out of blue chips. Not yet. There was another can't-miss quarterback—a Massachusetts kid, which made for a better story—and Barry had developed a close relationship with him, too. Then, one day, Steve Peach of Saugus, Mass., told Gallup he was very sorry, but that he was going to attend Syracuse.

It was that time. Three a.m., the coffee's cold and someone's stolen all the mugs. "Time to circle the wagons," as Bicknell would say. The one truism about football coaches held true: When their world is crumbling around them, they sit in their offices, in the dark, and watch more film. Four reels featuring one player waited on Gallup's desk. "Normally, you watch only one or two reels," Gallup said. "But he's the type of kid you have to see three or four times, because of his height." Gallup and Bicknell watched the kid throw a touchdown pass on one reel. He intercepted a pass on another. "Or he'd be scrambling or kicking a field goal," Gallup said. "We knew we had an athlete."

But could he be a quarterback? That was all 5-foot-9 Doug Flutie wanted to know when Bicknell and

Gallup visited his home that spring. "I remember Bill Bowes was waiting out in the driveway, hoping Doug would change his mind and want to go to New Hampshire," said Doug's father, Dick Flutie. "And I looked Jack straight in the eye, and I said. 'I don't think you know what you're getting.' "

3

Beginnings

The Flutie family's history in football was brief. Edward Flutie (Doug's grandfather) had played. It had been a wonderful experience. His nose had been broken more than once. His bones creaked years afterward. So when Edward Flutie's son, Richard (who would be Doug's father), bounced into their Baltimore home one afternoon and said he wanted to play high school football, Edward Flutie said, "No football."

Dick Flutie tried the next best thing. He played the organ. Richard Flutie and His (six-man) Orchestra played for Spiro Agnew, and for Baltimore Colts coach Don Shula. "We had a chance to be on the Merv Griffin Show," Flutie told the *Middlesex News*, "but got bumped by Lionel Hampton."

He dreamed of a family band (The Flutie 5?) while his children took music lessons. But when the Fluties moved to Melbourne Beach, Fla., his three sons began liking sports more than the trumpet. When his boys wanted to play football and the other sports, Dick sent off for the *Sports Illustrated* teaching series. "I don't clutter my mind with things I can look up," Dick Flutie said. He coached the kids himself.

Some things the books didn't discuss. For instance, his 8-year-old son Doug wanted to score a touchdown while his Midget League team was kicking off. "Run down the field, strip the ball from the return man and keep on running for a touchdown," Dick Flutie said. "Never been done down there." Then Doug did it.

No one had broken the Fluties' grandfather clock until Doug's younger brother Darren did it. With a baseball. Three times in three weeks. "Chandeliers, hanging lamps, coffee tables," Joan Flutie said. "It's hard to remember the first thing they broke, because they broke everything."

"Doug always had to be playing," said Bill Flutie, the oldest brother. "He used to make up games, and they were serious games. Hall football. Cup baseball. Crush a snow-cone cup, hit it with your hand and go around the bases."

Dick emphasized winning. "It never really was hard work," Doug said. "We just loved it. My father always pushed us to win. Some people might say that's the wrong thing to do, but it makes you do the things you have to do to win, and learn how to win."

Doug won. In a baseball all-star game in Florida, shortstop Flutie took a ground ball, faked a throw to first and dived to tag out the man trying to take third base. Doug was Most Valuable Player of that game.

"You know Kathy Johnson, the Olympic gymnast?" Joan Flutie said. "She and Doug grew up together in Melbourne Beach. While Doug would be up at bat, she was balancing on the outfield fence, doing back-flips and scaring everyone to death."

The games didn't change when Dick, a high-tech engineer, moved his family in 1976 to Natick, Massachusetts, a Boston suburb. Basketball was probably Doug's favorite sport. Once, his Natick High School team trailed by a point in the final second. Before Flutie inbounded, he stationed a teammate in front of him. "I'm going to run up and down the end line and run my defensive guy into you," Flutie said. "We're going to get the foul and the free throws without time running out."

"Well, he did it," Dick Flutie said. "The guy was knocked head over heels—and the official wasn't looking at the play. Boy, Doug was all over him leaving the gym."

"Watching Doug was always a thrill," Joan said. "Bill, our oldest son, always did very well. He got the play done. But even if Doug wasn't doing something *as right*, it would still be more fun to watch Doug play. Even if the others were better."

Doug built his reputation in football. "When he was in junior high, we had heard a lot about him," said Natick High School football coach Tom Lamb. "They said there was something special coming along."

Lamb promoted Flutie, a 5-foot-8 sophomore, to the varsity in August 1978, beginning him in the secondary of the second-string defense. The first-team offense didn't complete a pass against the second team in four days. "We couldn't overlook it anymore," Lamb said.

In the 1978 season opener, Flutie, the first-team 150-pound defensive back, blitzed. Suddenly, he was confronting a 210-pound fullback. "Somehow, Doug came out of the pile with the ball," Lamb said. "He ran all the way to the 15-yard-line. We scored and won the game, 6-0."

Doug replaced his brother, Bill, at quarterback that year. By graduation, he would earn eight varsity letters. He was a shortstop-pitcher in baseball, a Bay State League All-Star as point guard in basketball, and a two-time *Boston Globe* All-Scholastic in football, once as a defensive back, then as quarterback. "We didn't really have a good team around him, so we spent the first half following the game plan," Lamb said. "Eventually, we would go into the shotgun and let Doug throw every time."

The coaches let him control the game in other ways, too. "It was his sophomore year," Dick Flutie said. Natick led Braintree High School by two touchdowns before Braintree scored 15 points to lead, 25-24, in the final minutes. Doug passed four times to his brother, Bill, taking Natick to the 21-yard-line with 3 seconds left. A timeout was called before the field goal. "Let me kick it," Flutie said. He had never kicked in a game before. On the sideline, he tried to pull off his football shoe—to put on the kicking shoe—but there was a big knot in the lace. Teammates and coaches scrambled to pull off the shoe. Joan Flutie ran underneath the stands. "She was so excited," Dick said. She missed Doug's game-winning 38-yard-field goal. Bill Flutie was the holder. And Doug, by the way, was wearing the kicking shoe.

4

Recruiting

Flutie listed an 'A' average on college questionnaires, an interest in computer science, and several awards, leadership and excellence in three sports. BC had recruited him during the football season, inviting him to the 1980 Stanford game. "When BC beat John Elway, the big crowd was going crazy," Dick said. "And Doug said to me, 'If I get an offer here, this is where I want to go.' "

"We had been to a game at Brown (where Bill Flutie was a receiver) that morning," Joan added. "The difference between those two games was amazing. At BC we said, 'This is a football game.' At Brown, the women came in wearing their mink coats. It was disgusting."

The decision was made. "I was Boston College all the way," Flutie said. But his future was lost sometime that winter. BC head coach Chlebek stopped recruiting Flutie. Something about height, apparently.

"Height?" Flutie said. "I never even thought about height."

He was left to consider Holy Cross, which ended every season with a game against BC. "The first thing I wanted to do was go to Holy Cross and play BC and beat 'em," Flutie said.

One day, he had a phone message: Call Holy Cross. It was time to arrange his campus visit. "He called collect, the way he had been told to on these recruiting things," Joan Flutie said. "The guy who answered on the other phone said, 'I don't know any Doug Flutie; I've never heard of him,' and he refused to accept the charges. When Doug told Dick about it, Dick said, 'That's the end of Holy Cross.' "

Flutie later received a letter from Holy Cross, informing him he hadn't been admitted.

So he was left to consider Harvard, Brown, and the University of New Hampshire. UNH looked like a good choice. He liked the campus. Bill Bowes had indicated Flutie would have a chance at playing quarterback. And the Ivy League rules prohibited athletic scholarships. One morning, his father showed Flutie a newspaper story. Ed Chlebek had quit BC. "I didn't even read the article," Flutie said.

Two myths have been added to this legend. The first is that new coach Bicknell didn't recruit Flutie until after BC's favorite quarterback prospects—Muldoon and Peach—decided upon other schools. "Even if we had signed those two," said Gallup, "we probably still would have signed Dougie. As an athlete." And because they couldn't sign anyone else.

Myth No. 2 is that BC offered Flutie its last scholarship of 1981. He was among the final third to sign. "I was pretty low on their list," Flutie said. "At least, that's the impression I got."

Bicknell didn't offer the scholarship until Flutie visited the campus on January 30. He was promised a chance at quarterback. "But if it comes down to being the second-string quarterback or the first-string safety," Gallup told him, "you might want to switch." Negotiations concluded, Flutie signed the only Division 1-A scholarship offered him.

He soon received what appeared to be a letter of confirmation from BC. It turned out to be a letter of apology from BC's admissions office. Sorry, it read, but you will not be admitted into BC.

"The Fluties called, all upset," Gallup said. "It turned out to be a computer error."

Now that he had his first freshman class, Bicknell's next job was to evaluate his players, decide who could play which positions. "I don't mean to promote myself," Bicknell had said at his first BC press conference, "but I can tell (recognize) a football player, both in recruiting and on the field. There are some guys around who look like Tarzan but play like Jane."

And in the last few years, when asked how he knew Flutie could play quarterback, Bicknell referred to the June 1981 Shriners Classic high school all-star game, in which Flutie led the South to a surprising 21-16 win against the North, which had been a two-touchdown favorite. "You could see he was absolutely in control of that game," Bicknell has said. "He just took over. I said that night, 'We're not going to be moving him from quarterback.'"

But when Flutie arrived at his first preseason camp in August, he was listed as flanker. Though he threw with the quarterbacks in preseason practice, "I had convinced myself that I wasn't going to be a quarterback," he said. "I thought I'd be a defensive back or split end. It didn't matter as long as I could play major college football."

*   *   *

Overall, it was a bad recruiting year. The new staff was at least a month behind the other schools. When the "high-priority" recruits began choosing other schools, Gallup scrambled for what was left.

One was lineman Mark Bardwell of Methuen, Massachusetts. Yankee Conference coaches, including Maine assistant coach Mike Maser (who was now with Bicknell at BC), had recruited him. BC's Chlebek had held off because Bardwell was only 6-foot-1; potentially, he wasn't great. But Bicknell visited his home late in recruiting season and made his sales pitch.

"I see, coach," Bardwell said when Bicknell was done. "But what's important to me is that I'm your No. 1 recruit. All these other schools say I'm their No. 1 recruit."

"You want to be the No. 1 recruit?" Bicknell said. "Fine. You're the No. 1 recruit. You can be anything you want. I don't care."

Mark Bardwell signed.

One night during halftime of a BC basketball game, Gallup introduced Scott Gieselman, a 6-foot-5, 200-pound tight end from Weston, Mass., to Bicknell. Gallup had figured Gieselman might want to attend BC and walk-on to the football team.

Gieselman, obviously stunned, walked out of Bicknell's office after a 10-minute visit.

"What's wrong?" Gallup said.

"He just offered me a scholarship," Gieselman said.

"He *what*?" Gallup said.

Gallup barged into his office.

"You didn't offer him a scholarship, did you?" Gallup asked.

"Sure," Bicknell said. "The kid's 6-5. We have five scholarships left. Why not?"

If Gallup ever knew he was having a bad recruiting year, it was the night his head coach offered a scholarship to a non-recruited tight end he had never seen play, not even on film.

"We were one of the worst freshmen classes to come in here," Flutie said. "We saw that we were scheduled to play Alabama in 1983, and we laughed.

"Then we sat down and remembered we were going to be the juniors and seniors then. *We* were going to be the guys playing Alabama."

*　　*　　*

In August, Gallup assigned Flutie to room with Gerard Phelan, a fifth-string freshman tailback. They would talk about the season between practices.

"Think we'll make the travel team?" Phelan would ask.

"It doesn't look like it this year," Flutie would answer.

They agreed they'd probably be allowed to travel with the team as sophomores, then play regularly as juniors.

Phelan had been the tailback in a running offense at high school in Rosemont, Pa. But he caught anything thrown near him during practice warmups. "Keep catching the ball like that," Gallup said, "and we'll move you to receiver."

In BC's season opener against Texas A&M, Gallup sent Phelan the receiver in with a play on third-and-long. It was a surprise.

"What the hell is Phelan doing in there?" quarterback coach Tom Coughlin yelled into his pressbox phone.

Phelan caught a 17-yard pass for the first down.

"Nice substitution, coach," Bicknell told Gallup.

Meanwhile, Flutie, the backup punt-returner, called for a fair catch against A&M. "If you've got someone you think is going to be a star quarterback for you, you don't have him returning punts," Gallup said. "Obviously, we didn't know what we had."

But they knew what they needed: Someone to complete passes, even despite their surprising 13-12 win against A&M. First-string junior quarterback John Loughery had thrown six days a week during the summer, arriving at camp five pounds heavier but with a smaller waistline. But he suffered a thumb injury before the opener, so 6-foot-5 junior Doug Guyer started at quarterback for the first time since four years earlier in high school. Unsuccessful, he was replaced by senior Dennis Scala, the best thrower. He was no better, taking BC 94 yards before intentionally grounding the ball. "I saw something that I never saw before," Bicknell said. "That's when we drove from our 3 to their 8 and ended up punting."

By then, Phelan had moved out of his dorm room. "Gerard was interested in partying a little bit, having fun at college," Gallup said. "But after about a month, he said, 'Coach, Doug's so straight. His mother's there all the time. I can't enjoy myself. I feel like I'm at home right now.' "

Phelan told Flutie that a friend from home had invited him to move in. "In a sense, I ditched him (Flutie)," Phelan said. "I didn't even know him."

The next week the 16-point BC underdogs flew to Chapel Hill, where ninth-ranked North Carolina had beaten its first two opponents 105-7. After that third game, North Carolina had outscored the opposition 161-21, including the second-most points ever against BC, 56-14. Late in the third period, when North Carolina led

BC, 49-7, Tar Heel coach Dick Crum sent in his Heisman Trophy candidate, tailback Kelvin Bryant, to allow him to score his 15th touchdown in three games. Across the field, Bicknell shook his head and made a questioning gesture with his hands.

"No, I wasn't resentful," he said. "That's his business. I was just questioning why he would do that. If I were in his place? No, I wouldn't do it. They still have eight, nine games left and the kid might get injured."

"I think we owe it to Kelvin in a televised game like this to let him display the things he can do," Crum said.

Flutie was watching the sequence from the sidelines. Afterward, the upperclassmen reminded him and other freshmen to get revenge when BC and North Carolina played again in 1984.

The game was so bad that BC cheerleader Marie Houle, attempted a sideline handstand, suffered knee ligament injuries and was on crutches after the game. "It was a mismatch," Bicknell said.

There were others. The next week, West Virginia beat the Eagles 38-10. The NCAA would rate BC's schedule the third toughest in the nation.

"Our biggest problem is at quarterback," Bicknell said. Scala had suffered a badly bruised shoulder against North Carolina. Loughery had recovered and started against West Virginia, but was ineffective. "I just hope we have a healthy quarterback situation for Penn State Saturday," Bicknell said. "Because we have to throw the ball down there. That's for sure."

5

Penn State

Bicknell could look at it this way. Second-ranked Penn State had been favored to win by 24 points. The Nittany Lions led BC, 24-0, at the half. So in effect, the game was even.

Another perspective: In the last 10 quarters, BC had been outscored 118-24. That was the way Jack Bicknell saw it.

He met with quarterback coach Tom Coughlin and Barry Gallup at halftime in the visitors' locker room at Penn State's Beaver Stadium. "If things don't go a lot better in the third quarter," Bicknell said, "why not?"

Gallup took Flutie aside. "I said to him, 'Doug, you'd better be ready. I think you're going to get a shot,'" Gallup recalled. "I could see him getting excited."

Once the season had begun, there had been enough time during the week for only the first three quarterbacks to practice. So Flutie, the fourth-string quarterback, hadn't practiced since preseason. He wasn't used to it. "We knew it was hard for Doug," said his brother, Darren, "because he'd never not played."

So difficult that he was going to remain at quarterback two weeks more, he had decided, "at the most." Then he would request a move to receiver.

But that was history. Now Penn State was scoring its second touchdown of the half to take 38-0 lead into the fourth quarter. Flutie was throwing to a teammate on the sideline.

"Warming up, you could see he was getting more and more excited," Gallup would remember. "He wasn't thinking about 85,000 people at Penn State (at 84,473, it was the largest crowd BC had played before). He was just having fun."

"Doug," Gallup told him, "you're going to go in the first series of the fourth quarter."

Loughery had gained two yards on 15 passes in the first three quarters. BC had the ball on its 22 in the fourth.

"Tom," Bicknell said on the phone to Coughlin in the pressbox, "let's go with the kid."

Agreed.

"OK, Flutie," Bicknell said. "See what you can do."

On the radio, it was announced that Doug Flutie was the new Boston College quarterback. Joan Flutie was listening to the radio with her mother in Baltimore.

"Mother, mother, come here quick," Joan said. "Doug's in the game!"

"Well, you knew he was going to play," her mother said.

"Yeah," Joan said, "but not today!"

They sat in front of the radio.

On third down, he attempted his first pass: a 15-yard completion to Brian Brennan. Another third down: An 18-yard draw to Howie Brown.

He was moving them.

In Baltimore, Joan's mother whispered between plays, "Does Penn State have its second-string in?"

"Probably," Joan said, "but who cares?"

On the sideline, Gallup nodded to Flutie, who was waiting for a play on the field. "It was a 'Good job, let's go!' kind of thing," Gallup said. "In the middle of it, he winked at me. Here's a freshman in his first game, and he's winking. I couldn't believe it. I started laughing."

Flutie began to throw on first down. A 20-yard pass to Kevin Benjamin brought BC to the Penn State 23.

"I watched the kid bring the ball down the field," Phelan remembered. "I said, 'Maybe it's against the second team.' Then I said, 'It doesn't matter if it's against the second team. He's moving the ball. I want to be a part of that.' " He couldn't, because he was recovering from a sprained ankle.

"It was like somebody hit a switch and the tempo picked up," Bicknell said. "Never, ever, ever could we imagine what we had."

First down. Tight end Scott Nizolek cut diagonally toward the left corner of the end zone. Flutie led him to the goal line. The ball cleared linebacker Jeff Hochberg. Flutie was 3 of 3 for 58 yards and a touchdown, career.

"It was like, 'Oh my God, I don't believe it,' " Flutie said. "I had so much nervous energy it was ridiculous. I got out there and tried to remember plays. I wasn't reading coverages. I would just go back and pass and remember where the receivers were going. Most of the time, they were a little open."

They were open for 135 yards until his final play. Near the goal line, Flutie convinced Bicknell to change a play. He wanted to pass on fourth down. Flutie passed. Hochberg intercepted at the 2-yard-line.

"Coach Bicknell was mad at me after the game," Flutie said.

"If I was mad then, it was because I was saying 'We'll call the plays, and you do what we tell you to do,' " Bicknell said in the 1984 preseason. "Of course, now we say, 'You do what you think we should do.' "

Loughery sat with junior receiver Jon Schoen on the bus ride to the airport after the 38-7 loss. "John was saying, 'Sure, the kid came in and did a good job. He was impressive. But I'll be back next week,' " Schoen said. "And I was listening to him and saying to myself, 'I don't know . . .' "

*   *   *

Bicknell wasn't so sure. "I didn't think this was some magic thing," he would say. "I didn't say, 'OK, he's my quarterback of the future.' I just figured he'd done enough to deserve another chance . . . then another chance . . . then another chance. Eventually, I knew he was going to be the guy."

Flutie started for the first time the following week and lost, 25-10, to Navy. Then he completed 15 of 21 passes for 244 yards and three touchdowns to beat Army, 41-6. In the previous five games, BC had scored only 54 points.

"Flutie showed some things," Bicknell admitted after the Army game. "We've been trying to bring him along as a young quarterback, and he showed some things today."

Just in time. The following Saturday, No. 2 Pittsburgh and quarterback Dan Marino was scheduled to visit Alumni Stadium.

Pitt built a 29-10 lead early in the second half. Then Flutie drove the Eagles 88 yards, ending the third quarter with a 30-yard touchdown pass to Rob Rikard. 29-17.

Pitt fumbled at its 22, and in two plays, Flutie threw 17 yards to Rikard. 29-24.

Students could be seen leaving their dorms, coming to the stadium . . . just in case.

"I can't believe it," Joan Flutie said in the stands to Dick. "He looks like he's out there, playing with his brothers. I've been watching this all my life."

The latecomers had already missed a Flutie underhand pass, but they were in time to watch BC gain three chances to win. Halfway into the fourth quarter, the Eagles had first-and-goal at the Pitt 8, but BC's Geoff Townsend fumbled. No matter. With 4½ minutes left, BC had first-and-goal from the Pitt 9 yard line. A holding penalty lost 10 yards. Flutie was sacked to Pitt's 23. And BC's John Cooper missed a field goal.

It was a 29-24 loss, but it was also Flutie completing 23 of 42 for 347 yards and two touchdowns. In his third collegiate start, he had played the second-best statistical game in BC history. Against the nation's No. 1 rated defense.

"I didn't think that much about who we were playing and about any of that stuff about me against Marino until this morning," Flutie said after the game. "Then I was looking at the matchups in the paper. I saw 'Marino, 6-feet-4' and 'Marino, something like 40 pounds more' than me, and I said 'Hmmm.'

"Not in my wildest dreams did I ever think I'd be here."

"You look at him, look at his poise for being so young, look at the things he does and just hope we don't ruin him," Bicknell said that afternoon. "He believes in everything he does. He's flipping the ball around, doing some really goofy things . . . and they work. You watch him and just hope you don't coach all that out of him.

"If anyone told me that we'd get 347 yards passing against Pitt, I'd tell them they were crazy. I knew we had the ability for a good air game, but not to that degree."

"Flutie gives us an intangible element," Gallup said. "With him in there, we felt we could make the big plays on offense. With him, I think this team grew up today."

*   *   *

But then came word that Flutie had been injured against Pitt. A knee strain. "I won't use him unless he's completely healthy," Bicknell said. "Because of his size, Doug needs plenty of leg movement. He can't see over those big on-rushing linemen. He has to scramble or pick up his receivers looking through cracks . . . We won't play Flutie at 85 percent, because without his feet he's a sitting duck."

Flutie started. BC beat Massachusetts, 52-22.

This was followed by a reminder that he was still just a freshman surrounded by unproven teammates. Ahead, 7-3, in the first half, BC had first-and-goal at the Syracuse 3 yard line. An offsides penalty pushed the Eagles to the 8. Flutie pitched the ball too high for tailback Steve Strachan, who bobbled the ball and was tackled at the 16. Flutie was sacked (one of eight times), and Cooper missed a 41-yard field goal. "From seven points to nothing," Bicknell said. "There are so many things I don't understand. We rushed for 260 yards and Doug Flutie connected for 224 yards." And Syracuse recovered in the second half to win, 27-17.

Two weeks later, Flutie finished his first season with a 25-yard pass into the corner of the Holy Cross end zone, where BC's Scott Nizolek and Holy Cross' Bill

McGovern were waiting. "There was no spiral on the ball but it fluttered down there," Flutie said. "I thought the ball was intercepted before I saw the official with his arms signalling touchdown."

It had been an interception, momentarily. Then Nizolek pulled the ball from McGovern and, with 3:48 left in the game, fell on his back with the winning touchdown. BC beat Holy Cross, 28-24, and Flutie (251 yards and two touchdown passes) won the O'Melia Award as the game's outstanding player.

BC and its first-year coach finished 5-6. The Eagles won four of their last six games with a freshman quarterback, and nearly beat the No. 2 team in the nation.

"You know, I learned something from Pitt," Bicknell said. "Man for man, I didn't think they were all that good and I don't think (Pitt coach) Jackie Sherrill did, either. But the sons of guns, they went out on the field and they expected to win. It made me realize that the difference between the real good teams and teams like ourselves is not that great. It is simply in how the kids look at themselves."

With that, he announced that the competition to be starting quarterback in 1982 would be wide open, despite Flutie's No. 9 ranking among the nation's QBs. "That's the way is has to be," Bicknell said. "John Loughery (the backup quarterback Flutie replaced) is a potential captain next year. He has to be given a chance. So do the rest."

6

Clemson

Flutie won the starting quarterback job for his sophomore season, but was his an enviable position? The NCAA had ranked Boston College's 1982 schedule as the fifth-toughest in the nation. "I feel we have the people to be a better team than last year's," Flutie said. "Take me, for example. I wasn't even in the picture at the start of last season and I got to start the fifth game."

Flutie was responsible for a couple of changes. Doug Guyer, who had started BC's season opener at quarterback a year ago when freshman Flutie was fourth-string, had gained 20 pounds and become a first-string defensive end. And Reid Oslin, BC's assistant athletic director for sports publicity, had decided to publish mini-biographies of each freshman in the BC football media guide. Like the other freshmen, Flutie had been mentioned only on the roster of the previous year's media guide (and then he was carelessly listed as 5-foot-10). That had not satisfied public demand. "We never had a freshman come in like Doug," Oslin said. If BC brought in another, Oslin would be ready.

But the most significant change affecting BC had occurred in College Station, Texas, where former Pittsburgh coach Jackie Sherrill had signed a six-year, $1.7 million contract to coach Texas A&M. No person in an American university was earning as much as Sherrill for

work performed on university assignment. His new
A&M regime would begin September 4 against Boston
College. In Texas.

"We've been practicing in 105-degree temperatures,
and down on the turf, I figure it's around 140 degrees,"
Sherrill said before the BC game. "But don't worry. By
game time (7 p.m.). it'll be 94 degrees and cool."

Jack Bicknell worried about the Texas weather
more than having to play a Sherrill-coached team.
Mainly because of their new coach, the Aggies (who
were 7-5 the year before Sherrill arrived) had been rated
between No. 10 and No. 19 in almost every preseason
ranking. "It's hard to believe you can get a Top 10
ranking just on the basis of hiring a coach," Bicknell
said. Nonetheless, unranked BC—which had beaten
A&M the previous year—was a 15-point underdog.

The Eagles flew some 2,000 miles to Houston the
day before the game, then bused 90 minutes to A&M. It
was raining. So they bused another hour to practice at a
dry site. They didn't eat dinner until 9 p.m.

It was 91 degrees when the game began the following night. The Eagles' bench was on the sunny side of
Kyle Field. The Aggies sat in the shade, with built-in air
conditioners at their backs. "Let's put it this way,"
Sherrill said of the air conditioning. "The guy who sup-
plies it is an Aggie."

A&M fumbled on its first offensive series, and BC's
Guyer recovered at the Eagle 49 yard line. Flutie (who
had been remeasured and found to be 5-foot-9½) then
passed 45 yards to Jon Shoen for a 7-0 lead.

The Aggies kicked a field goal, but Flutie completed a 55-yarder to Brian Brennan, setting up Flutie's
8-yard naked bootleg into the end zone. It was 14-3 in

the first quarter, 24-6 at the half. By then Flutie had completed 11 of 17 passes for 211 yards.

His first pass of the second half was intercepted and A&M closed to within 24-16. Flutie then threw a 32-yard touchdown to Brennan. That finished the Aggies. BC 38, Texas A&M 16.

It was a stunning victory. Flutie completed 18 of 26 for 356 yards and three touchdown passes, each TD resulting from his having changed the play at the line of scrimmage. He had seen a lot of the same defensive schemes as a freshman, when he played Sherrill's Pittsburgh team. Still, the Eagles were admittedly shocked at how well they had moved the ball. "We were taking what they gave us," Flutie said. "But I don't know why Texas A&M was running the kind of defense they did. It was very unsound."

"Nobody said it would be easy," Sherrill said.

Certainly, nobody at BC had said that. But it had turned out that way, and when practice resumed the following Tuesday, Bicknell wanted to make sure his players knew the next game would be tougher. "This week I'm gonna run the players right into the ground," Bicknell said. "My thinking now is that we'll bust their humps this week."

They had two weeks to prepare for their next game, at Clemson, the defending national champions.

*   *   *

The A&M victory carried them through the next few days. The BC coaches wrote on a blackboard. "Jack's pennies beat Jackie's millions. We want a raise."

Bill Flynn, the BC athletic director, laughed with them. "By the way, Sherrill's the AD at A&M, too," Flynn said. "How about me getting a raise?"

In a strange way, Flynn was as responsible for the sudden success as anyone. For years he had scheduled BC against Stanford and Texas and other national powers. And he had been criticized, not necessarily for scheduling great teams, but for not giving his own BC teams an equal chance to win. BC's facilities, support staff, coaches' salaries, and recruiting budget couldn't match those of some of the teams the Eagles played every year.

But Flynn could never be accused of trying to sabotage the football program. He played end and captained the 1938 BC football team, and earned nine varsity letters upon graduating in 1939. After serving four years in the FBI, he taught math at BC, worked for BC's Alumni Association, and was an assistant BC football coach. On July 1, 1957, he was named BC's athletic director.

He was elected president of the NCAA (while remaining as BC's AD) in 1979. He survived the basketball team's point-shaving scandal of the 1970s. So he could withstand criticisms of his football schedules, which he kept, handwritten, on notepaper in his breast pocket. He always said that a college football program could survive in a pro-sports town like Boston only if the top teams came to town once in a while. But the obvious complaint was the Bald Eagles' cry that no BC football team had played in a bowl game during the 25 years Bill Flynn had been athletic director.

Now the pieces seemed to be fitting together. He had hired Bicknell because he liked Bicknell's offensive style—it would create interest. They had been fortunate, finding this kid Flutie. People liked to watch him play, and he was a pretty good quarterback. Perhaps the key factor was the NCAA's reclassification of football schools after the 1981 season. Boston College had been designated the only Division 1-A, major college football school in New England. If the good New England players wanted to stay close to home, they would have to attend BC. The football program was suddenly in an excellent situation.

The next critical step was this game, at Clemson. It was a regional TV game. If BC could play respectably, and if Flutie could look good, then this would be a football program carrying a lot of momentum. But if the defending national champions blew the Eagles away, then 1982 would be the 40th consecutive disappointing season.

Clemson was known as "Death Valley." The nickname began when a piece of stone from the original Death Valley was placed on a pedestal above one end zone. Clemson players rubbed the rock for good luck before they ran onto the field. A crowd of 63,000, wearing mainly orange, packed Memorial Stadium for every game. This Eagles' team had never experienced anything like this.

Bicknell didn't want them going in unaware, so he blasted rock music from the Alumni Stadium sound system during practices. "It was the worst music I ever heard, and our BC neighbors didn't appreciate it," Bicknell said. "But we had to get our players used to the noise they'd face in Memorial Stadium."

Flutie didn't mind it. "It makes you concentrate harder," he said. "Everyone's mind stays on the practice. And the guys on the sideline can enjoy the music." Also, he learned his signal-calling could beat the noise. "For a small kid," he said, "I have a big mouth."

The Eagles arrived in Clemson, South Carolina, the Friday before the game and visited the stadium. They brought their cameras, posing around the rock and in front of the Tiger paws painted about the stadium.

And while the Clemson Tigers were running down the ramp Saturday afternoon, the BC (12-point underdog) Eagles were on the field, watching. "It was the first time we'd been introduced to it," Flutie said. "We decided we wanted to be out there. We had heard so much about it, and coach Bicknell figures, 'What the heck? Let's be out there.' A lot of coaches had warned him about being intimidated by that. I guess nothing really intimidates this team with our attitude. It's a very loose attitude. We don't care. We can go play anywhere."

Could they? BC trailed 14-0 after two quarters. Flutie had thrown two interceptions and had lost a fumble at the Clemson 11. The game had the makings of BC's blowout loss at North Carolina the year before. "We had been wiped out at North Carolina," Bicknell said. "The team let down during the game. I didn't know which direction we were going. And you can be sure I was thinking of that when we went to halftime at Clemson trailing 14-0."

There, he decided to run the ball, to relieve pressure on Flutie.

The Eagles drove 72 yards for a touchdown on their first possession of the second half. Sixty-two were gained on the ground, the last 11 by freshman tailback Troy Stradford, who fumbled, recovered the ball, then re-fumbled shortly after crossing the goal line.

Flutie began the fourth quarter with a four-play, 61-yard drive. On third-and-short from his 47, he noticed Clemson had only two defensive backs deep. Flutie changed the play at the line, sending three receivers into the area. Scott Nizolek was left open for a 36-yard pass, and Flutie quickly threw to Jon Schoen in the right corner of the end zone to tie the game at 14-14.

BC kicked off. Clemson fumbled. BC's Kevin Snow kicked a 37-yard field goal. The Eagles led, 17-14, and hadn't allowed Clemson past midfield in the second half.

Clemson's Donald Igwebuike kicked a 43-yard field goal to retie it.

Then Flutie began BC's final drive. He ran for 20 yards and passed for 12 yards twice. It was first down at the Clemson 23.

"We wanted a touchdown," Bicknell said, reconstructing the drive. "I didn't think a field goal would be good enough for the win. I was watching those guys, the Clemson kickers, in pregame warmups and they were putting on the greatest kicking exhibition I'd ever seen. We didn't want to give them a chance at the end."

Flutie was supposed to throw a quick down and out, but he was bumped out of the pocket. Rolling to his right, he motioned with his left hand to receiver Paul Zdanek. Zdanek broke upfield. He was alone.

Flutie overthrew him.

"Oh, wow," Flutie would say after the game. "How did I do that? He was there. I just didn't get the ball to him."

A Bob Biestek draw play gained four yards. On third and six, when most coaches would have run the ball, hoping for the best but settling for the field goal attempt, Bicknell wanted to pass. His assistants on the phone discussed the possibility of a sack that could ruin a field goal attempt, but they agreed they had to go for the touchdown.

"We called the same pass pattern we used for a touchdown to Jon Schoen," Barry Gallup said. "It's the safest play we have. On every other pass, there is a blocking mismatch, but in this one, all the backs are blocking, every possible rusher is covered. It's the best protection we have against a sack."

BC left offensive tackle Gary Kowalski slipped and fell when the play began. Clemson defensive tackle Jim Scott ran past him. "My back was to him," Flutie said. "I never saw him. I was looking to make the pass. It was open."

But he was sacked for a nine yard loss, and Kevin Snow missed a 50-yard field goal.

There was 2:22 left and now Clemson was driving to win. When eight seconds remained, Igwebuike was ready to kick his second 43-yard field goal of the game. BC called a timeout to let him think about it. Igwebuike missed the field goal.

The BC locker room was quiet after the game. "A tie is all right," Flutie said. "But we should have won the game. We had our chances."

Those outside the locker room thought a BC tie at Clemson was remarkable. The national media became interested. ABC's Jack Whitaker arrived at BC to tape a report on Flutie. A TV crew followed him to classes. *The New York Times* wanted to do a story. A national following had begun.

Bill Flynn said these were the best back-to-back football games in his school's history.

7

Comeback

The next challenge was avoiding a BC letdown. The Eagles' history of colossal flops was founded in losses to Temple in 1974, Tulane in 1975, and Villanova in 1976 and 1980. And even in 1981, after beating Texas A&M, BC had that blow-out at North Carolina.

"I could be sitting here 0-2," Jack Bicknell said on the plane to Baltimore and BC's third consecutive road game, against the Naval Academy. "You don't want to blow this week and have the things you've done the first two weeks not mean the same. So many good things have happened, we don't want to let it get away. Nobody on this team has ever beaten Navy (the Midshipmen had beaten BC each of the last three years) and our kids know that."

"I think we've eliminated the fear of your basic BC letdown," said BC junior linebacker Steve DeOssie. "I feel more pressure on this game to win. I see this as a bigger game. If we lose, Clemson and Texas A&M don't mean a thing."

Flutie's new national prominence also concerned Bicknell. "I never realized before what it must be like at some of those places (with star players)," Bicknell said. "The media's been around all week and it does place demands on Flutie's time. It's partly because he's small and he's exciting."

And he was good, throwing for 279 yards and three touchdowns at Navy. But the Eagles fumbled seven times. "I started to get discouraged when we were fumbling," Flutie admitted. "The defense kept us in the game."

The Eagles were beginning to sound as if they expected to win every game. Amazingly, they were unhappy with the offense after a 31-0 victory against Navy.

"I hope this will silence the few critics we have," DeOssie said. "That should silence the last of them."

DeOssie was one of the few highly recruited Eagles, having turned down scholarship offers from Notre Dame, Wake Forest and Miami. Harvard wanted him too, but DeOssie didn't seem like the Ivy League type. He admitted to participating in barroom fights and he shaved his head during football season. Despite his 250 pounds, he was quick and the key to a defense that funneled running plays to the linebackers. And he was becoming a leader, standing over tackled ball carriers, his fists raised, screaming. DeOssie's teammates soon learned to celebrate tackles the same way.

The Eagles were ranked in the Top 20 in the Associated Press and United Press International weekly football polls when BC (2-0-1) played Temple. In a 20-minute period, Flutie threw nine straight incompletions. "I had no spiral on it," he said. Also, the BC band drew a 10-yard delay-of-game penalty for an overly-long rendition of "Alleluia Chorus."

However, Flutie began the second half with four straight completions, and he finished with 18 of 36 for 256 yards (but he lost his best receiver, Brian Brennan, to a broken collarbone). Meanwhile, BC's defense had allowed 10 points in 10 quarters when the 17-7 victory against Temple was finished.

The week before No. 19 BC played at No. 16 West Virginia, the Bald Eagles were squawking. One afternoon, Bicknell received a call from Rev. Maurice Dullea, S.J., who had captained the 1916 Eagles' football team and had been the BC athletic moderator who hired Frank Leahy.

"He didn't even say hello," Bicknell said. "He said, 'This is Father Dullea and let me just tell you two things. One, they're going to be talking Flutie for the Heisman. Just tell him not to pay any attention to it. The other thing they're going to be saying is, here's the Sugar Bowl, and you just tell them to see you after the Holy Cross game (the final regular season game) when they talk like that. That's all I've got to say to you, coach.' Then he just hung up."

It was Homecoming at West Virginia. Flutie suffered a minor thumb injury during the game. Though he would say afterward that it didn't have a great effect upon him, he completed only 9 of 33 for 122 yards and four interceptions (as many as he had thrown the first four games of the season), probably the worst game of his four-year college career.

BC trailed, 13-6, with 10:45 left in the game when West Virginia's Darryl Talley batted down Flutie's third-down pass at the BC 20, but a defensive holding penalty nullified the play and a BC drive began. Flutie threw to freshman tailback Troy Stradford, who ignored a shoulder injury and gained 45 yards to the West Virginia 25.

Three running plays left BC inside the 10, but Flutie was held short of the first down on a fourth-and-one play. No matter. An illegal motion penalty against BC forced the down to be replayed.

So, with 8:32 left, and fourth-and-goal at the 6, BC kicker Kevin Snow ran onto the field. But not to try a field goal.

"We'd been practicing the play all week," Bicknell said.

Holder John Loughery (the No. 1 QB before Flutie) took the snap, jumped up and rolled to the right. "We had noticed West Virginia rushed up the middle on field goals," Bicknell explained. Loughery threw to tight end Scott Nizolek as the play was designed. But . . . "as I was coming across, I got held by a defender and fell. Howie (Brown of BC) thought I was down for good, so he went for the ball and tipped it." Straight to Nizolek, who caught the ball while sliding.

It was 13-13—another dramatic BC tie—when Eagle defensive back George Radachowsky waited at his 13 to catch a West Virginia punt. He fumbled. West Virginia recovered. Mountaineer QB Jeff Hostetler scored in four plays. West Virginia 20, BC 13.

"I'm gonna play up the positive," Bicknell said. "I'm gonna tell the kids that it was our first loss in five games, that we've been on the road in four of those five games, and that we've played in three of the toughest places on the road and done well."

But Bicknell, too, was depressed. He sat through films of the dismal loss on Sunday. When he left his office that night, his car had been stolen.

This was going to be a lousy week.

*   *   *

However, Bicknell kept alive the company line. "We're not in awe of anybody anymore," he said. "I feel pretty good about the way they approach things.

Historically, the problem here has been never believing they belong in the Top 20. They're smart enough. They know they have to play well to beat Rutgers (a two-TD underdog). That's the point. They want to."

With 1:18 left, fans were leaving Alumni Stadium when Rutgers punted to BC's 13. The Eagles trailed, 13-6, and had to drive 87 yards in 78 seconds with no timeouts. In ran Doug Flutie, who had thrown four interceptions.

"Here's where I'm preparing my talk," Bicknell said. "I'm going to tell the players: 'Don't get down; we can still have a good season despite this loss.' Rutgers is thinking: 'Well, we've got this damn game won.' "

On first down, the Knights pressured Flutie as they had all game. Incomplete. Next he scrambled right and passed sidearm to Jon Schoen at the BC 37. "But we're still not going anywhere," Bicknell said.

Flutie threw out of bounds to stop the clock, then hit Scott Nizolek at the Rutgers 49. But a holding penalty pushed BC back to second and 20 at its 27. "Now we're dead," Bicknell said. "We're at midfield, we're driving, and then a penalty gets us back to the 27—it's not our day."

Here, Flutie threw one of his few good passes of the day (he would complete only 15 of 40 in the game), to Paul Zdanek over the middle. BC receiver Gerard Phelan was trying to block downfield when he saw a Scarlet Knight make the tackle as Zdanek caught the ball. "The ball bounced off the safety's helmet and went up in the air," Phelan said.

Phelan dived for it.

"As soon as I saw the ball pop in the air, all I thought was interception," Flutie said.

Instead, the Eagles had a first down at Rutgers' 47.

"I knew we were in trouble when he caught that," said Rutgers coach Frank Burns.

The clock stopped while the officials moved the down-and-distance chains. Less than 50 seconds remained. "Flutie's on his own," Bicknell said. "I had no control over the game, unless the ball went out of bounds to stop the clock."

Flutie dropped back to throw a screen left. He ran instead, stepping out at the 35. There, Rutgers linebacker Jim Dumont was penalized for a late-hit. First and 10 at the Rutgers 20. Less than 40 seconds left.

"On one play, we've come from nowhere to the point where we've got a chance to win," Bicknell said. "When we were on the 20, I knew we were going to score. Tom Coughlin (Bicknell's quarterback coach in the press box) and I were able to spend almost the rest of the time talking about what two-point play we might want to run."

"I stepped out of the huddle and said: 'Look where we are,' " recalled BC guard Glenn Reagan. " 'If we're this close, there's no way we're going to be stopped.' "

Flutie remained cool. "Once in a while that year Flutie would get a little uptight," Reagan said. "He would stumble over his words, or he might want to check something and say, 'Wait a minute.' The older guys would say, 'It's OK, cool down.' But our guys were very intense. There wasn't any talking in the huddle."

Flutie dropped back. Nearly sacked, he escaped and scrambled to the 5. He threw out of bounds again, stopping things at 24 seconds. It was second and goal at the 5.

Again, Rutgers pressured him and he ran out at the 2 with 16 seconds left.

The excitement in the stands matched the comeback on the field. "Everybody who left early to beat the traffic must have heard on the radio what was happening, because they came surging back in," said BC sports publicity director Reid Oslin.

Third and goal, and Bicknell was signaling Flutie to pass. Almost as he was turning from center, a defensive end was charging him. "I was just trying to make sure I didn't get sacked," Flutie said. "If you get sacked with the clock running, we're dead. I couldn't see Troy (tailback Stradford), but I knew he was one-on-one over there somewhere to the right. I just threw to the spot, thinking it would be incomplete."

He sidearmed a pass around the defensive end. Stradford turned at the goal line to see the ball in the air. "It was already halfway to me," he said. "Doug had to throw off of his back foot, so it was a floater behind me. I meant to stop, but my feet went out from under me. I reached up and tried to make a sliding catch while I was falling backward."

He caught it a few inches above the ground.

Flutie didn't know Stradford had scored until he saw an official raising his hands and his teammates' celebrations. "The place was in total pandemonium," BC assistant coach Coughlin said. "Jack asked me what the situation was. I said we up here feel we've gotta go for the win. Jack wasn't laughing, but he started giggling, and he kept saying, 'OK, OK, OK, OK . . .' "

"We went nuts," Stradford said. "People were jumping all over the place. A lot of people didn't realize we still had to score another two points for the win."

Flutie realized it. "Right away, he got an official and pointed to the right hashmark, telling him we wanted the ball there," Coughlin said.

BC prepared two two-point plays for each game. Bicknell decided to use an unbalanced line, five men to the left of center. "They're thinking we're going to run a sweep behind the left side of the line," Bicknell said. "We could have done that, but obviously our thought was to put the ball in Flutie's hands and win or lose with him."

He ran a naked bootleg right and saw Nizolek open in the end zone. "I short-armed it to him, like I was throwing darts," Flutie said.

"I've seen guys in the clutch choke and throw it in the dirt doing that," Bicknell said.

With 12 seconds left, BC led, 14-13. The scoreboard read: "This is a team of destiny."

"It was one of the great moments, if you understand the moment, the exhilaration of overcoming those odds," Coughlin said. "What would you say? A 95-to-1 shot? When we had no chance of winning, and then to win . . . we believe we can overcome anything if we don't give up."

The game had other impact. "If we had lost to Rutgers, we would not have gone to the Tangerine Bowl," Bicknell said. "If we win it, we're (eventually) 8-2-1 and a bowl team. If we lose, we're 7-3-1, nice try, but we'll see you later."

8

Tangerines

"The team is trying to think Army," said Jack Bicknell, "but is constantly hearing Penn State. I for one am scared stiff by a team like Army."

Flutie celebrated his 20th birthday by completing only 5 of his 16 passes with an interception while Army built a 14-12 lead. "Maybe we all expect too much," Bicknell said. "The guy is not perfect. But you've got to stick with him because he comes up with the big play when needed."

With 10 minutes left in the third quarter, Flutie threw 40 and 23 yard touchdown passes and BC beat Army at West Point, 32-17.

Now the Eagles could begin thinking about Penn State.

BC had lost all 10 games against Penn State, the first in 1949 and most recently in 1981, when Flutie had first appeared. But in this 1982 season, BC was 5-1-1, the game was at Alumni Stadium and the Eagles were, like Penn State, a possible bowl team. The seventh-ranked Nittany Lions (6-1) were only 8-point favorites.

Yes, the *serious* bowl talk had begun. If BC could just make a game of this one, stay close, the Eagles could for the first time in 40 years go to a you-know-what game.

"Bowls, bowls, all this talk about bowls," said BC defensive backs coach Pete Carmichael, laughing. "We're not sure how to take it. There's only one person on this squad or coaching staff who's ever been to a bowl and that's (quarterback coach) Tom Coughlin. He went once as a player and once as a coach (at Syracuse), but the rest of us have no idea. The closest we've been to a bowl is the one in the cafeteria with sugar in it."

This game had been sold out since September 21, the earliest a game had been sold-out in the 26-year history of Alumni Stadium. Athletic director Bill Flynn even tried to scrounge tickets from his head coach.

A top officer of a Boston bank called the BC football office, then the sports publicity department, offering $1,000 for four tickets to the Penn State game. "Do you think I could say to my wife," mused Bicknell, " 'Say, hon, you didn't really want to go to the Penn State game, did you?' "

The Eagles appeared to be peaking for this game. At least they felt they were. "I've had some zip on the ball this week," said Flutie, who had completed only 35 of 99 in his previous three games. "Not just me, but the whole team is excited about playing again and that's something that's been missing the last few weeks. I feel I perform better in a big game like this. It brings out the best in me. I don't know if it's good or bad, but when we play a lesser opponent, I don't play as well. A game like this . . . this is the reason you come to a school like BC. To play one of the best teams in the nation and test yourself against them and to see how good a team you really have."

A record Alumni Stadium crowd of 33,205 waited for the test results. Statistically, they were great—Flutie passed for 520 yards (best in the nation in 1982, and

10th-best in NCAA history) and BC gained 656 overall. But Penn State gained 618; worse, the Nittany Lions won, 52-17.

For the first time, Flutie (26 of 44) didn't wear a flak jacket. "That ball really was whistling on the field," Bicknell said. "His throwing technique, setting his feet, releasing from the top, his hip movement, all were perfect."

He completed 6 of his first 7 for 77 yards, a touchdown and a 7-0 BC lead. But Penn State's Kenny Jackson caught a 59-yard TD from Todd Blackledge to tie it, and tailback Curt Warner went on to gain 183 yards and three touchdowns. These three Nittany Lions would become first-round NFL draft choices.

"If you had told me before the game that they could score that many points, I'd say you were crazy," Bicknell said. "I honestly never have seen that many skill-position people on one field."

They were helped by a BC offense that ended most drives with fumbles (four for the game) or interceptions (two). "This is the craziest damn game I've ever seen," Bicknell said. "I'll say this, the 17 points is the absolute least we could have scored today."

The Eagles trailed, 38-17, with 10 minutes left. "I asked the coaches if we could go with the two-minute offense to see if we could get a couple of quick scores and get back in it. I thought we still had a chance despite the score."

BC didn't go into the quick no-huddle offense, which pleased Penn State. "I never want to stand on the sidelines through something like this again," said Paterno, who shook Flutie's hand after the game. "I'm ahead, 38-17, in the fourth quarter and I don't know whether I can get the second team in there."

"Sure, I wish we didn't have as many turnovers," Bicknell said. "But in our offense we are not going to be mistake-free. We are living with the pass to compete against these teams."

It was an exciting life.

*   *   *

The Eagles beat Massachusetts, 34-21, and then came word that a win the next week against Syracuse would ensure BC of a bowl bid. Three years earlier, the headline in the *Boston Sunday Globe* had read: "BC Sours Syracuse's Tangerine Bowl Dreams." Then, BC (2-6) had upset Syracuse (6-4) and ruined the Orangemen's hopes of playing in a bowl.

Now, BC (6-2-1) had to beat Syracuse, "the best 2-7 team in the country," according to Jack Bicknell.

Syracuse had recently beaten Colgate, 49-15, prompting Syracuse coach Dick MacPherson to say, "I see the light at the end of the tunnel, and it's not an oncoming train."

A BC assistant coach approached Bicknell. "He said, 'How about if we turn that line into a T-shirt?' " Bicknell recalled. "I wanted to motivate our kids. It was a game we had to win—a bowl bid was riding on it, and we were playing an extremely good team with a poor record."

Thursday before the game, BC coaches gave their players 90 orange T-shirts that read, "The Train."

"Everybody was hollering," said BC offensive tackle Mark MacDonald. "We needed something to psyche us up."

A heavy rain had subsided by kickoff, but a 20 miles per hour wind swept through Alumni Stadium, affecting each team's passing game and producing a hard-hitting game before a small crowd (21,500).

Syracuse outrushed BC, 282-205 yards, and led, 13-10, late in the third quarter. Flutie hadn't completed a pass in the first half, but on third and 8 from his 17, he dropped back, slipped and almost fell, scrambled right and somehow passed 26 yards to Paul Zdanek for the first down. The 85-yard drive ended with Kevin Snow's 27-yard field goal and a 13-13 tie with 11 minutes left.

The Orangemen recovered, moving 60 yards to the BC 3, where Eagle defensive back Tony Thurman recovered Glenn Moore's fumble. The officials huddled to decide whether Moore was down before fumbling; finally, they awarded the ball to the Eagles.

"The key play of the game on defense," Flutie said.

After Syracuse regained possession and missed a 47-yard field goal, it was Flutie's turn. A defensive holding penalty gave him first down at the BC 35. He threw a 21-yard pass to Paul Zdanek. Less than two minutes remained. Another pass.

"On the next one, (fullback Bob) Biestek wasn't even supposed to be out there," Flutie said. "But after my fake and bootleg, I saw the deep receiver wasn't open and neither was my end. I suddenly saw Bob (15 yards upfield) and he made a nice sliding catch."

First down at the Syracuse 29. Flutie checked the play at the line, sending Gerard Phelan on a jet pattern into the end zone. He stood alone behind his defender when Flutie threw.

"It seemed like an eternity," Phelan said. Should he run forward and jump for it? Or wait and hope the defender couldn't recover in time? The ball hit him before he could decide. He held it against his chest. His first touchdown catch came with 58 seconds left.

"That," Bicknell said, leaning against his office wall after the game, "could be our most important win since I've been around BC football."

The following Sunday night, near midnight, Bill Flynn unofficially accepted a bid to play in the Tangerine Bowl. He called Bicknell and told him to keep the news quiet.

"I came to BC with my son Jack (a guard on the BC football team) and I didn't say a word about it," Bicknell said. "I thought something was a bit different when I entered Roberts Center (home of BC's athletic offices). About 25 students were lined up at the ticket office to get tickets for Saturday's game with Holy Cross. All of them looked extra happy. And that was at about 7:30."

Then he walked into his office and read in the newspaper that BC would play Auburn in the Tangerine Bowl in Orlando, Florida. "I've told Jack (Bicknell) about it," Flynn was quoted as saying. "The kids have done a great job. They deserve this."

But they had also paid a price. Syracuse coach Dick MacPherson had learned of BC's orange T-shirts. At his Monday press conference in Syracuse, N.Y., he accused BC linebacker Steve DeOssie of cheap shots and made an angry promise. "They used a lot of crap to win that game," MacPherson said, referring to the shirts. "I'll tell you one thing. It'll be a long time before they beat us again."

*   *   *

Citrus fruit had never been so popular in New England. Dick Flutie, Doug's father, was answering his phone, "Hello. Tangerine Bowl Committee." Exams

were rescheduled to allow students and faculty to follow
the team to Orlando, resulting in the largest airlift of
people (10,000) from Boston to one destination since
World War II. Bicknell earned a new contract, and he
saw the Tangerine Bowl as a reward and a recruiting aid,
for the times he competed against Pitt or Penn State.
"They (the glamor schools) don't poor-mouth you, but
their coach is sitting there talking to the prospect and
the Gator Bowl watch is on his arm and the Sugar Bowl
ring is on his finger. He'll roll that gigantic national
championship ring over to the kid and say, 'How do you
like this?' And I'm sitting there with my wedding ring
on my finger and my Timex on my wrist. Now I'll have a
watch down at the Tangerine Bowl and when I go out
recruiting, I'll have my sleeve rolled up and that sucker
out there."

When the Eagles arrived in Florida, Flutie com-
mented during a press conference that he had returned
home, having grown up in Melbourne Beach, Florida.
And he revealed that he wore No. 22 because Joe Wiles,
a local high school player, wore it. When that news
reached Melbourne Beach, friends nicknamed Joe
Wiles "Idol."

The bowl-week was a new experience for both
teams. Bicknell and Auburn coach Pat Dye came to be
good friends. And though Auburn hadn't played in a
bowl since 1974, the Tigers obviously came from another football world.

"So how's your TV show doing?" Dye asked Bicknell during a banquet.

"What TV show?" Bicknell said.

BC tried to prepare for Auburn's wishbone, but the
practices in Orlando were low-key. "You're tired from all
the running around," Flutie said. "Plus it's hard to

think about football when you're going to Disney World in two hours. You find yourself thinking about Disney World."

Reporter Leigh Montville of *The Boston Globe*: "The most quiet trip was to the Kennedy Space Center. The players were stuffed into the buses, and tour guides at the front droned on about the weight of booster rockets and the cost of the space shuttle runway and the danger of all the fuels and the players started to doze.

"Then an alligator was spotted from a window.

" 'Hey, an alligator!'

" 'Gator!'

" 'Look at the gator!'

"The tour guide droned and the billions of dollars of technology stood at attention and everyone watched the alligator."

Jack Bicknell was asked if he could last through the daily banquets and activities for a year. "A year?" he said. "I don't know if I'll make the week."

At one press conference, Bicknell said the game would be "high-scoring." At another he said it would be "low-scoring." At a third he was asked if it would be "high-scoring" or "low-scoring."

"Probably somewhere in the middle," he said.

"So what is it?" a reporter asked after the final press conference of the week. "Which is it going to be?"

"How do I know?" Bicknell said. "They keep asking me that question, and how can anybody answer it? You have to play the game to find out."

It was high-scoring. Auburn led, 23-10, at halftime. "I hate to admit it, but I was tight the first half," said Flutie, who was 10 of 22 with two interceptions at halftime. "I was very average in the beginning of the game."

"I didn't expect Auburn's speed," Bicknell said.

The Eagles were killed by another short player, Auburn's 5-foot-7 Lionel James. "He made the single most important run of the game, in my opinion," Bicknell said. "In the fourth period, we scored to make it 33-18, plenty of time (nine minutes) left, and we've got them pinned, third and 11, down on their 7 yard line.

"Third and 11! And they run the option, and James goes 12 yards around his left side. I knew then we were out of business."

With 2:29 left, Flutie returned to the sideline after BC's final fumble, slamming his gold helmet and then himself on the BC bench. A minute later he was standing, calling for a timeout.

"Call it," he told Bicknell. "Maybe we can score another touchdown."

Bicknell called it. Auburn fumbled on the next play, and Flutie took the Eagles into the end zone in the final 46 seconds. Hundreds of fans ran onto the field and BC waited six minutes until the people could be cleared away. "When we finally huddled up, I looked out there and Auburn had two assistant coaches in the defensive huddle," Bicknell said. "I said: 'Go ahead and run it anyway. Those guys aren't wearing pads.' "

Flutie ran in the 2-point conversion, spiking the ball in the end zone.

"There, again, he knew exactly what he was doing," Bicknell said. "He knew it was illegal, but he also knew there wasn't any time left. He just wanted to show his frustration, just wanted to let it out."

BC (8-3-1 in 1982) had lost, 33-26. "That was important in my mind, to have a final score that truly reflected the game," Bicknell said. "We didn't win but we played the game. We wanted to make the Top 20 and we won't. So we're 25th nationally. Hey, if you'd told me last September 3 (before they opened the season at Texas A&M) we could be 25th, I would have said, 'I'll take it. Put it in writing and just tell me where I sign.' "

"You know, it's just been wonderful," Dick Flutie said. "Coming down here for the week. Enjoying everything. Seeing what we've seen. You just wish it would last forever."

Forever, no. Two more years, yes.

9

Break

The bowl game had created a more hectic off season in 1983. LSU coach Jerry Stovall and Florida State assistant (and ex-BC quarterback) Mike Kruczek attended BC's spring practice to study the Eagles' passing game. Offered $600,000 by CBS, athletic director Bill Flynn agreed to switch BC's game with Alabama to November 25 when it could be televised nationally. But this left the Eagles with two weeks off in the middle of the season. And Flynn had trouble coming up with a season-opening opponent, signing Division 2 Morgan State in the late spring.

Doug Flutie earned $7 an hour the summer before his junior year installing the new SuperTurf at Alumni Stadium. He took summer courses to stay ahead and changed his major from computer science to communications, taking advantage of his media experiences. He also became the first New Englander and the second junior (the first was Georgia's Herschel Walker) to join ABC's nationwide, eight-cities-in-eight-days college football promotional tour. Senior linebacker and tri-captain Steve DeOssie lost 15 pounds to improve his quickness, and BC doubled season ticket sales to more than 10,000.

BC coach Jack Bicknell said the offensive line and quarterback were his concerns. "Doug could twist his ankle tomorrow," Bicknell said. "If he goes down, you don't want the team to say, 'Oh, jeez, we can't win now.' Last year we had two seniors backing up a sophomore. This year coach (Tom) Coughlin is coaching nine quarterbacks. It's gonna be like The Gong Show. We're going to bring 'em in and whoosh."

Bicknell was also concerned with the statements coming out of Morgan State in Baltimore. "Some people say we're crazy (for playing BC)," said Morgan State athletic director Tom Dean. "You'll find out we're not when we're riding back from Boston with a win."

"We're going to win," promised Morgan State first-year coach James Phillips, who put his team through three practices a day, including, he claimed, an 8-mile morning run. "Football is not hard. I've been doing it all my life."

"He's unbelievable," Bicknell said. "It scares me. He's predicted in writing, three separate times, that Morgan State is going to beat BC. Maybe they know something we don't know."

The Morgan State Bears' buses were held up in traffic and didn't arrive in Boston until 4 a.m. on game day. BC then beat them, 45-12. The most memorable play was in the second quarter, when Flutie was sacked by one Bear and "the other guy (freshman linebacker Jeff Greene) was holding my ankle," said Flutie, who broke Frank Harris' BC record of 4,555 career passing yards. "He started to twist it and I kicked him trying to get away. When I kicked at him, he retaliated." He jumped on Flutie and the officials kicked Greene out of the game, but not before a fight began near the Morgan State bench. "We don't like people jumping on Flutie," said BC offensive tackle Mark MacDonald.

"What I don't want is our kids turning into a vigilante committee," said Bicknell, who almost fainted on the sideline due to a chest cold. "Against Clemson, a 15-yard penalty could lose the game for us."

Yes, Clemson was coming to Chestnut Hill for a rematch. The Tigers, on NCAA probation, promised a "10-man rush of Flutie": They would rotate 10 linemen to maintain a fresh, four-man rush. Clemson was the winningest team in the nation (22-1-1) since the start of its 1981 national championship season and advertised its defensive line as the nation's best, including 6-foot-3, 320-pound nose guard William "Refrigerator" Perry, who could stuff a basketball. Four thousand Clemson fans were expected to join their team, with 375 planning to stay at the Newton Corner Howard Johnson's motel, whose sports coordinator, Joel Broudy, was worried. He had read that "Tiger Paws are painted all over the roads to Clemson," Broudy said. "Our general manager wouldn't be too happy with Tiger Paws all over the place."

BC turnovers allowed Clemson a 13-3 halftime lead, 16-3 in the third quarter. But it would have been worse had the Eagles not held the Tigers to three field goals in TD situations. "The thing about the first half was that we were running the ball well then, too," said BC sophomore tailback Troy Stradford. "We were just fumbling and making mistakes."

"We needed to get the ball down there and finish off with a touchdown," Flutie said. "That was the feeling. Score a touchdown and everything would open up."

Stradford carried the ball off right tackle from the BC 32. The left side, where the play was designed to go, was jammed. The right side was open. "I've never seen that before," he said. "I just went for it. The referee got in my way for a half-second, but I got away from him and got moving." He didn't stop until he had gained 43 yards and had started the comeback.

They ran four more times before Flutie threw a 6-yard touchdown pass to tight end Scott Gieselman. The Eagles had made their statement. They were going to keep the ball on the ground.

Despite Steve DeOssie's badly bruised left shoulder (he ran with his arm at his side), Clemson didn't score again. The Eagles scored six minutes later to take the lead.

In the fourth quarter, Flutie rolled right while two Tigers chased him. He relaxed as if content to run out of bounds—the Tigers relaxed too—then threw to Gerard Phelan, who slid for the first-down catch. "I was just trying to throw the ball away," Flutie said, "but at someone." Flutie audibled the next play, clearing Phelan for one-on-one coverage and the 39-yard touchdown pass that clinched this 31-16 victory.

More impressive than Flutie's passing (20 of 36 for 223 yards and two TDs) was BC's running: 281 yards against Clemson. Despite being acclimated to the humidity of the early September evening, and even with 10 men shuffling in, the Tigers were obviously exhausted by the end of the game. "We formationed them," said BC quarterback coach Tom Coughlin. "We put ourselves in a situation where we were strategically better off and able to run the ball." Clemson was never able to react to BC's unbalanced lines and blocking schemes, and Alumni Stadium had probably never been louder.

"It's funny how people think," Flutie said. "They think that to be a powerhouse, you have to be a running team. They somehow think a passing team isn't legitimate. I never have thought that way, but I guess there can't be any complaints now."

Not on the night the New Year's Day bowl talk began.

1982 photograph of Doug Flutie as a sophomore.
(GLOBE PHOTO BY FRANK O'BRIEN.)

Doug Flutie's parents in their Natick home. (GLOBE PHOTO BY JOHN BLANDING.)

Mr. & Mrs. Flutie move through a crowd after 1984 game. (GLOBE PHOTO BY JOHN BLANDING.)

Doug Flutie (22) passes in the first quarter of the
Liberty Bowl in 1983. (GLOBE PHOTO BY TOM LANDERS.)

Quarterback Doug Flutie shuffles off a pass just in
time to avoid a West Carolina defender in Boston
College 1984 win. (GLOBE PHOTO BY MARK CARDWELL.)

Flutie unleashes the first of his three first-half touchdown passes in the first quarter against North Carolina at Sullivan Stadium in 1984. (A.P.)

West Virginia defensive players Matt Smith (50), Scott Dixon (59) and David Grant (98) celebrate, following a sack of Doug Flutie (22) late in the fourth quarter. W.V.U. won 21-20. (A.P.)

Rutgers' Jack LaPrarie tries his
best to catch Doug Flutie. (GLOBE
PHOTO BY JANET KNOTT.)

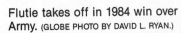
Flutie takes off in 1984 win over
Army. (GLOBE PHOTO BY DAVID L. RYAN.)

Doug Flutie (22) hands off to Troy Stradford in third quarter of Syracuse game in 1984. (GLOBE PHOTO BY JOHN BLANDING.)

Having some fun, Doug Flutie warms up left-handed in early 1984. (GLOBE PHOTO BY FRANK O'BRIEN.)

Quarterbacks Bernie Kosar of Miami and Doug Flutie meet just prior to the 47-45 win by B.C. (A.P.) ▶

Doug Flutie directs his receivers with his left hand as he scrambles to complete a second-quarter pass against the Hurricanes in the Orange Bowl, 1984. (U.P.I.)

Wide receiver Gerard Phelan (20) prepares to haul in a touchdown pass from Doug Flutie to win, 47-45. Miami defenders try in vain to block or deflect The Pass. (A.P.)

Flutie exults after the final Miami score. (JIM BULMAN—FROM TELEVISION COVERAGE.)

Boston College players
fall on top of each
other in excitement
after The Pass
beats the Miami
Hurricanes. (A.P.)

Gerard Phelan demonstrates
his joy following The Catch.
(U.P.I.)

Doug Flutie is greeted by his two nieces upon his
return, at Logan Airport, after win against Miami.
(GLOBE PHOTO BY MICHAEL QUAN.)

B.C. coach Jack Bicknell holds up cowboy
boots he received from the Cotton Bowl
committee. (GLOBE PHOTO BY FRANK O'BRIEN.)

Large Boston College crowd awaits official Cotton
Bowl announcement by B.C. President, Reverend J.
Donald Monan, S.J. (GLOBE PHOTO BY FRANK O'BRIEN.)

Mayor Ed Koch clowns with Doug Flutie at New
York City Hall reception. (GLOBE PHOTO BY JIM WILSON.)

Doug Flutie admires his trophy before the
Heisman dinner at the New York Hilton Hotel.
(GLOBE PHOTO BY JOHN TLUMACKI.)

Doug Flutie and a Massachusetts state trooper watch the clock run out on Houston. (GLOBE PHOTO BY JOHN BLANDING.)

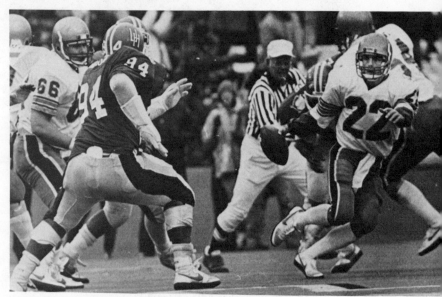

Doug Flutie scrambles as Houston nose guard Eddie Gilmore (44) attempts to tackle him during the Cotton Bowl action. (GLOBE PHOTO BY GEORGE RIZER.)

An enthusiastic Boston College alumnus at the 1984 Cotton Bowl game against Houston. (GLOBE PHOTO BY JOHN BLANDING.)

The happy quarterback eats a sandwich in the crowded locker room after the Cotton Bowl victory. (GLOBE PHOTO BY GEORGE RIZER.)

Doug Flutie holds the Cotton Bowl trophy after the win over the University of Houston. (GLOBE PHOTO BY JOHN BLANDING.)

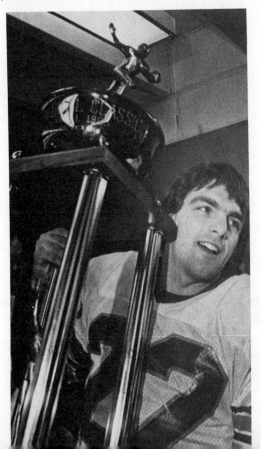

*   *   *

Flutie was named NBC's "Sportsman of the Week" and was interviewed on the Today show. ABC and CBS made arrangements for live interviews Saturday afternoon in New York, before BC's night game against Rutgers at Giants Stadium.

The CBS limousine arrived at BC's hotel before noon, whisking Flutie off to midtown Manhattan and Brent Musburger. Brent asked Flutie about his lack of height. Flutie said he wasn't the "stereotypical" quarterback.

"That's the first time," said CBS sports president Neil Pilsen, "we've ever heard a college football player use the word 'stereotypical.' "

Waiting at the hotel was an ABC remote crew, which presented a live remote interview with ABC's Jack Whitaker, who had discovered Flutie a year earlier. "We still feel we're one of the best teams in the East, if not the best," said Flutie, setting unofficial TV records as the first collegian on two network pregame shows the same day, and on all three networks in the same week. "But right now we're worrying about Rutgers. Rutgers is tonight."

There wasn't much to worry about. Flutie completed six of eight passes for 139 yards and a 19-3 BC lead in the second quarter. That was when Bicknell signaled a running play to Flutie and drew no response from his quarterback. Timeout.

Flutie was incoherent.

"Hey, Shawn," Bicknell yelled to second-string quarterback Shawn Halloran. "Get your hat."

A Scarlet Knight had kneed Flutie's helmet at the end of a scramble. The quarterback was feeling the effects of a mild concussion. "Heads," said Bicknell, who removed Flutie from the game. "You don't mess with heads."

"He was acting very confused," said Dr. Dennis Griffin, a BC team physician.

It turned out he had played much of the first quarter and all of the second in a daze. He was led to the bench, a towel around his neck, and sat with BC junior student-trainer Joe Patten.

Flutie jumped up. Patten jumped up and pushed him back down to the bench. Flutie jumped up again. "I didn't know where I was," he said, "but I wanted to get back in there." He was pushed down again. Patten had his orders.

This went on for several minutes. "He didn't know what was happening but he still wanted to go back in," Patten said. "When I asked him the score, he had to look up at the scoreboard to tell me."

Meanwhile, Shawn Halloran was proving BC had at least a competent backup quarterback, completing 8 of 12 for 102 yards and his first touchdown. Before Halloran could finish his 42-22 win, Flutie had returned to the field for the second half, still wearing his football pants. "He told me at the half," said Patten, " 'If we fall behind, sneak my equipment back onto the field.' "

*   *   *

Flutie appeared clearheaded after the game, though his memory had failed him.

"I ran the ball about 14 yards, put my head down and was popped," Flutie said, recreating the injury. "It was the first quarter and . . ."

No, Doug, he was told. It was the first play of the second quarter.

"No, it was the first quarter."

Second quarter.

"It was the second quarter?"

How do you feel now?

"Right now I feel fine," he said. "I think."

Doctors told Bicknell that Flutie would be recovered in time to play against West Virginia the following Saturday. Bicknell was getting tired of talking about injuries.

"I said last week Flutie's only a twisted ankle away from not playing," Bicknell said. "The bookies got hold of it and we must have had five or six calls last week about Flutie's twisted ankle. Don't these guys read the papers?"

If they were interested in Flutie, they had to begin reading *Sports Illustrated*, too. That week, he became the first BC athlete to appear on the cover (although an Eagle basketball jersey had been featured the week *Sports Illustrated* wrote about BC's point-shaving scandal). If BC had wanted to pay commercial rates for the advertising Flutie had brought the school through network TV and the *Sports Illustrated* cover those last two weeks, it would have cost *$850,000.*

Still, Flutie's head and the fabled cover jinx were the least of his worries. In the distance was that darned two-week layoff. "I've called all over the country and no one knows how to handle it," Bicknell said. "I think the key is having a good record before the break. If we go into it while we're down, it'll be awful."

There were other BC injuries. Steve DeOssie had missed the Rutgers game due to his bruised shoulder, but would probably play against West Virginia. And starting fullback and tri-captain Bob Biestek had suffered a broken wrist against Rutgers and was out.

Then there was the opponent. West Virginia (3-0) was ranked 12th in the country and senior quarterback Jeff Hostetler looked like a first-round draft choice. BC (3-0) was 19th in the nation. ABC was televising it to 35 percent of the country.

BC won the coin toss, and Stradford received the opening kickoff, turned upfield and was tackled unconscious by West Virginia's West Turner. The Mountaineers recovered Stradford's fumble and led, 7-0, 87 seconds into the game. When Stradford tried to return to the field, he couldn't move his leg. He had suffered strained knee ligaments.

"Losing your doggone starting tailback the first play of the game, that's mean," Bicknell said. "When he fumbles the ball I'm sick to my stomach, and then to find out he's out two to three weeks makes me want to throw up."

Three minutes later, the Mountaineers noticed an alignment mistake in BC's defense and ran a fake-punt 67 yards to lead 14-0. After BC wasted five scoring plays inside West Virginia's 5 yard line, Mountaineer flanker Gary Mullen ran a reverse on third and 13 for a 15-yard touchdown and a 24-3 lead, 24-10 at the half.

Overall, the Eagles would have 14 plays five yards or closer from the goal line, and score only twice. Bicknell would blame the officials for missing two touchdowns. "But all I can sound like is a crybaby," Bicknell said after the 27-17 loss. "I just don't want to take anything away from West Virginia, and I don't want to cry in my beer." Anyway, his team had still made a game of it.

It was 27-17 when Flutie (23 of 51 for 418 yards and three interceptions, eight rushes for 60 yards) passed

BC to the West Virginia 5 with five minutes left. Flutie started to roll out when "a cornerback came up and contained me," he said. "So I pulled up and looked for Scott (Gieselman) coming across the end zone. I tried to lob it back to him but I didn't put enough on it."

West Virginia's Anthony Daniels stepped back, jumped and intercepted him and began to run. Flutie dived and yanked the ball from him. It bounced to BC tackle Shawn Regent, whose hands were taped. "I couldn't even feel it," Regent said. West Virginia recovered.

BC regained possession at the Mountaineer 42 with 4:01 left, and in four plays Flutie had thrown a touchdown to Joe Giaquinto. Bicknell was planning a 2-point conversion and onsides kick when the touchdown was nullified by a holding penalty that ABC commentator Frank Broyles said was a "ridiculous" call by the official.

So for the second straight year, Bicknell had to avoid a letdown the week after losing his first game of the year to West Virginia. This time the opponent was Temple, before 7,033 at Franklin Field.

Temple led BC, 15-10, with eight minutes left.

With Stradford's injury, sophomore Ken Bell was BC's new No. 1 tailback. Bell was now set to receive Temple's kickoff in the fourth quarter.

"All week I was telling Bucky Godbolt, who coaches our special teams, that if Bell goes down running back kickoffs (like Stradford) to have a car waiting because you and I are going to disappear," Bicknell said. "You and I won't be able to go back to Boston."

Bell returned the kick 51 yards to Temple's 47. Three minutes later, Flutie faced fourth down at Temple's 4 yard line. He was supposed to keep the ball, but when an Owl was pulling him down, Flutie chest-passed a lateral to tailback Steve Strachan, who fell over the goal line. BC noseguard Mike Ruth came up with the game-winning sack that pushed Temple out of field-goal range. Temple coach Bruce Arians would later complain that Strachan had stepped out of bounds before scoring.

Cowboy Jack was laughing afterward. "We dodged a bullet, pardner," he said. "Doug Flutie doesn't always do what he's supposed to do. Thank God."

A 42-7 win at Yale the following week left the Eagles with a 5-1 record and two weeks to wait before Penn State.

10

Blackout

The two-weekend layoff allowed Boston College assistant coaches to recruit out-of-town, and tailback Troy Stradford, fullback Bob Biestek, linebacker Steve DeOssie and receiver Gerard Phelan to recover from injuries. When everyone was back and ready for the October 29 resumption of the schedule, Penn State had become the best team in the East.

The Nittany Lions who had beaten BC 52-17 while winning the 1982 national championship had been bludgeoned in their first three games of 1983. Then they had recovered to win five straight, including games against Alabama and West Virginia when each was ranked in the Top Four. So now No. 19 BC (5-1) vs. Penn State (5-3) was being played before a Sullivan Stadium crowd of 56,188 and a network TV audience. "If we lose, the sun's still gonna come up," Jack Bicknell said. "But it's gonna be more difficult. We've been given a second chance to do something."

Steve DeOssie felt extra pressure. "I haven't been playing as well as I can," he said. "Sometimes the guys look to me to get them excited. I feel a lot of personal responsibility for this game."

Bicknell had decided to take the Eagles through a week of conditioning and a few days of back-to-basics practices while his coaches were away recruiting. Then BC resumed a regular game week. Crazy. How would the Eagles play after 20 days without a game?

Well, they drove 80 yards to begin the game with a 7-0 lead.

"I don't think we had any doubts in our minds going in about being rusty," Bob Biestek said. "After a while, you don't want to hit your own people."

"We knew we weren't going to be rusty," Flutie said. "How can you be rusty after three weeks of practice?"

Flutie then threw a 25-yarder to Brian Brennan, who tipped it as he was hit at the Penn State 42 by defender Mark Fruehan. The ball deflected to BC's Troy Stradford, who was—fortunately for the Eagles—out of position. He ran 34 yards for 14-0. "When I saw that happen," Flutie said, "I had a feeling it was going to be our day."

The Eagles partially blocked a punt, Flutie threw 32 yards to Brennan and Steve Strachan ran the final four. It was 21-0 with 11 minutes left in the first half.

Meanwhile, BC's defense was constantly blitzing Penn State quarterback Doug Strang. It hurt only when Strang didn't have the ball. Tailback D.J. Dozier took a handoff and ran through the blitz untouched 42 yards for a touchdown and a 24-10 score at halftime.

Flutie carried a streak of nine straight incompletions in the second half when Penn State began to blitz, too. So when Strang threw a 20-yard touchdown, it was a close 24-17 with 7:41 left in the game and BC was facing the wind.

No matter. "We were grinding it out—through passing," said Flutie (24 of 43 for 380 yards, two TDs and an interception). "You can control the ball through the air efficiently, and that's what we did." They retained their daring: Flutie led Phelan down the sideline for a memorable 29-yard diving catch that symbolized BC's style. Four more passes took BC to the Penn State 20, but Flutie was sacked at the 23. With Kevin Snow's 40-yard field goal, the Eagles celebrated their first win ever against Penn State.

On the sideline after the 27-17 victory, Steve DeOssie was screaming, arms extended, helmet in hand, head shaven. *Boston Globe* photographer Frank O'Brien noticed him and sprinting across the field . . . too late. DeOssie was standing, dazed.

"Scream, Steve!" O'Brien ordered.

DeOssie reverted to form. It was a wonderful picture.

*   *   *

And a wonderful victory. "The biggest," Bicknell said. "Just because Penn State has always been the team in the East you had to beat, and now we've done it."

"Penn State," Flutie said. "We're on a level with Penn State."

The bowls were chasing BC now. The New Year's Day Fiesta Bowl of Tempe, Arizona, reported the Eagles were one of several teams under consideration, and the intermediate bowls were extremely interested. The bowl talk grew louder each day, and not just because BC was 7-1 and ranked No. 13 after beating Army, 34-14. A major reason was Flutie: some 20 minutes after the Army game, he was still on the field, signing autographs for 50 fans. One handed Flutie a football. Flutie threw him a pass. Hit the kid in the gut. He was magic.

His coach was flustered. "We were not flat," Bicknell said after the Army win. "What I really think is that the kids read all the crap about bowls all week and nobody talks about Army. Nobody talks about winning that game. They talk about all that stupid stuff. What bowl are we going to go to, what the situation is. It's stupid stuff right now. Well, from now on we're not going to talk about that. We're only going to talk about Syracuse."

That was fine, since Syracuse was only talking about BC.

Syracuse coach Dick MacPherson had not forgotten what had become the Choo-Choo T-Shirt Caper. Bicknell said he never understood why MacPherson was so upset. "I felt badly that it was misinterpreted," Bicknell said. "I wasn't trying to make fun of them. I never once thought he'd find out, or that if he did find out, he would take it the way he did. I have no problem with Dick. I hope he doesn't with me."

MacPherson, a former coach at the University of Massachusetts, wouldn't comment. "To bring other things into it (the game) would be wrong on my part," he said. But during the previous summer, he had admitted privately that he was still mad at Bicknell. It had gotten so bad that MacPherson's wife wouldn't speak with Bicknell's wife. It was a prolonged misunderstanding that made no sense.

Friday night before the game, while BC athletic director Bill Flynn was entertaining representatives from five bowl games at Mario's restaurant in Syracuse, MacPherson promised supporters that Syracuse would beat BC.

Unknown at the time, Flutie had entered a slump. "I had gotten away with it at Army," he would say later. "It's little habits you fall into, lazy things. Rather than springing back to pass, I was taking my time, sliding back. When I'm really on a roll, I lean backward as I'm dropping back, then step up, lean (almost bouncing) forward and throw. But when it was taking me so long to drop back, when the receivers were getting open, I was still on my back foot. So I ended up throwing off my back foot."

The bowl representatives watched Syracuse knock down Flutie's first two passes, force a punt, then drive for a 7-0 Orangemen lead.

The 41,225 fans in the Carrier Dome were already loud. The Orangemen were jamming BC's receivers at the line while pressuring Flutie with a four-man rush. The package was ruining BC's timing. Syracuse led, 14-7, at the half.

The Eagles made it 14-10 in the third quarter. And then three bowl reps stood up to leave. "We have to go back for our meetings tomorrow," said Tom Fridena, a thin, tanned real-estate broker, and a member of the Fiesta Bowl team selection committee. He was the key bowl person.

A limousine was waiting outside the Carrier Dome. The bowl people got inside and listened to the game on the radio. "And that's the end of the third quarter with the score Syracuse 14, Boston College 10," said the radio announcer. "A win here for Syracuse would be its biggest since the last game of the year against West Virginia two years ago."

"It certainly would," his partner said. "Boston College is ranked 12th, and Boston College is looking for the bowls."

The limousine stopped at the hotel. The bowl people got into their rental cars and drove to the airport.

Fridena turned on his radio and heard Flutie throw a third-and-10 completion with 9:55 left.

"Nobody ever remembers the scores or anything," Fridena said. "It's just the record going in. This has been a thriller."

BC held Syracuse.

"They've gotta do it now," Fridena said.

Troy Stradford ran to Syracuse's 26. He would gain 147 yards. BC called a timeout, fourth and four at the 20 yard line, 5:50 left.

Flutie, who was 2 of 10 so far in the second half, dropped back.

"Don't throw, don't throw," Fridena said.

He threw.

"Intercepted!" yelled the radio announcer.

"Doggone it," Fridena said. "Intercepted. That's the ballgame. Son of a gun, I thought they were going to win it."

In the airport, he sat down and dropped a quarter into a TV.

"Here," he said. "Syracuse 21, BC 10. Final."

He appeared stunned.

"This is a bad day for the Fiesta Bowl," Fridena said.

*   *   *

It wasn't so hot for the Eagles, either. Flutie was 12 of 36 for 114 yards and three interceptions. "I have to keep telling people," Bicknell said. "The kid is just a kid."

That night, the chartered plane scheduled to carry Bill Flynn, BC support staff, alumni and media members skidded to a halt on the runway at the Syracuse airport.

"Folks, this is Captain Cash," the pilot announced. "We have a slight problem. We hope to have it under control in a few minutes."

The cabin began to fill with smoke.

"Folks, this is Captain Cash," he said. "We have a slight problem with the hydraulic system. That's the reason I had to stop the plane with the emergency brake system. I'm going outside to see if we can't rectify the situation."

The co-pilot later said that if the plane had taken off, all emergency backup systems would have required them to land. So Flynn waited four hours while another plane was brought in, and the following day he waited by the phone while the bowls invited teams.

That Sunday night, November 16, the Liberty Bowl of Memphis, Tennessee, was trying to invite Alabama and Notre Dame, but Alabama refused. Overtures were made to Oklahoma, but Notre Dame preferred to play BC. So the Liberty Bowl would be BC vs. Notre Dame, the only two Catholic universities playing major college football. "I'm thinking of converting, it sounds so good to me," Bicknell said.

When BC beat Holy Cross, 47-7, and Flutie recovered from his slump (despite a sore arm that forced him to stop throwing on the Thursday before the game), BC officially accepted the Liberty Bowl bid. But in South Bend, Indiana, Notre Dame lost to Air Force, and the Irish (6-5) were no longer sure they wanted to play in a bowl game, forcing the Liberty Bowl to wait two days before finally accepting the bid. The Bowl claimed it was pleased with Notre Dame's decision, but the Irish had tarnished the Liberty Bowl's 25th anniversary game.

No. 15 BC (8-2) still had another to play—the Thanksgiving weekend national TV game against No.

13 Alabama (7-2) at Sullivan Stadium. "I hope it snows two feet in Boston," said Alabama coach Ray Perkins, hoping to stop BC's passing game.

Perkins got a little snow . . . and rain . . . sleet . . . 19 mph winds.

And a blackout.

At 3:12 p.m., halftime, with the game tied, 6-6, the wind felled a tree on Elm Street some three miles from the stadium. The tree landed on a transformer feeder line. The scoreboard lights went out, pressbox phones connecting coaches died, CBS' TV cameras were rendered useless, and two concessions workers were trapped in an elevator. New England Patriots owner and stadium namesake Billy Sullivan was moments from boarding an elevator himself when the Blackout Bowl began. "We had guys changing shirts at halftime because it was so wet," said BC defensive end David Thomas. "They had to bring lanterns into the locker room for us."

The game resumed as scheduled. Officials kept time on the field and CBS broadcast a radio play-by-play with a "Please Stand By" logo. TV viewers missed a blocked BC punt that Alabama returned 52 yards for a touchdown and a 13-6 lead. "After the block, it was dark and all, but we were saying if the fans in the stands had to hold candles, we would stay and we would win," Bob Biestek said. "You know Doug isn't going to stay down all day."

But if the fans weren't going to hold candles, the officials were getting ready to call the game on account of darkness. The team that was ahead at dusk would win. Then the power returned at 3:55 p.m., and BC's third goal line stand of the game prevented the Crimson Tide from adding to its lead. The Eagles were playing other games, too. "Every once in a while, one of them (from Alabama) would say, 'Boy, it sure is cold,'" and we would say, 'Hey, we're having a warm spell here,' " said DeOssie. He pointed to his bare midriff and claimed to have torn the midsection from his jersey at halftime. "Just to give them something to think about," he said.

His teammates were more sensible. "Throwing, I felt fine," said Flutie (14 of 29 for 198 yards, a TD and an interception). "But it was so bad that when you came out of the game after not moving the ball you were almost glad because you had a chance to get warm."

In the fourth quarter, the Crimson Tide fumbled twice inside its 35 (they had six fumbles overall). BC scored both times to win, 20-13.

In one season, Boston College (9-2) had beaten Clemson, Penn State and Alabama. The Eagles now had a chance to add Notre Dame to that list. "Last year, the thrill was getting to a bowl," Bicknell said. "It was our first in 40 years. But we didn't win. This year, the thrill is to win."

11

Heisman?

The long 1983 regular season had been replaced by the break before the bowl game. Time to relax, to study, right?

Then the Downtown Athletic Club called.

"The Heisman people have asked him to be there," BC sports publicity director Reid Oslin said in late November. "They bring in the top candidates every year."

Nebraska running back Mike Rozier, Brigham Young quarterback Steve Young and BC's Doug Flutie were the three top candidates. Flutie was the only junior.

This was the best indication that he would be *the* top Heisman Trophy Candidate early in 1984.

It was difficult to pin down the method of earning the Heisman Trophy. Since 1970, every winner except halfback George Rogers (1980) of South Carolina had played for teams ranked in the final Top 14, whose games had been televised by network TV at least twice. A good team legitimized the candidate and the TV appearances exposed his skills to the nation. Television was the dominant factor, though most of the 1,050 voters worked for newspapers.

Based upon that formula, an extravagant publicity package was not absolutely necessary. Especially for Flutie.

"My standing joke is that I've had a Heisman budget of $23 this year," Oslin said. "That covered the cost of Xeroxing a picture of Doug and stapling it to some updates of his statistics.

"Everywhere we play, all the media wants to know about Doug. I tell the writers we have Brian Brennan here, a terrific receiver, has broken all the school records. The writers say, 'Fine, what time does Doug get here?' I say we have Steve DeOssie, a great linebacker, shaves his head, a true wildman. The writers say, 'Very interesting, now where's Doug?' That's just the way it is."

Doug's brother Darren was a running back of the Natick High School team playing in the state Super Bowl on December 3, the same day as the Heisman announcement. His parents had decided to attend the high school Super Bowl.

If Flutie won the Heisman . . .

"My God," said his father, Dick Flutie. "I'd croak."

But Flutie knew he wasn't going to win. "And he wanted to see Darren play.

"Do I have to go to the Heisman thing?" Flutie asked assistant coach Barry Gallup.

"What do you mean, do you have to go?" Gallup said. "Of course you have to go."

Once there, he was glad he had come. The hour before the announcement, he, Young and Rozier waited in a room. "Doug and I are similar in so many ways that we hit it off immediately," said Young, who finished second in the Heisman voting with 153 first-place votes to Rozier (482). "We must be the only two college players in America who don't drink."

"I glanced at Mike Rozier when they announced his name," said Flutie, who drew 23 first-place votes to finish third. "I must admit it would be nice to win."

*   *   *

BC's recruiting had improved. "Everybody knows about us now," said Bicknell, who announced he was recruiting Darren Flutie. "Maybe it's because of Flutie, or the Alabama game where the lights went out, or maybe because we beat Penn State."

One thing was sure: The Liberty Bowl wasn't helping as much as No. 13 BC had hoped. Notre Dame and its beleaguered coach Gerry Faust were 6-5, and admittedly had been invited because the Fighting Irish always drew good TV ratings.

"They (the Irish) are the ones with everything to gain and nothing to lose," Steve DeOssie said. "We're the ones with everything to lose and nothing to gain. Our team goal is to be ranked as high as we can. We want to go into the Top 10. The only way we can benefit by winning is to win soundly. If we win, 22-20, that's not enough. We've got to win by at least two or three touchdowns if it's going to help us."

The Alabama game had been good practice for the Liberty Bowl. When the BC plane landed December 23, two hours late, it was 18 degrees and the ice was inches thick on the Memphis streets. Six BC luggage bags were missing.

The Eagles rushed off to Memphis State University to get in the day's practice. The grass field was frozen and a cold wind pelted them with snow. When Brian Waldron tried to kick his first Memphis field goal, he slipped on the ice and landed on his back.

"A week ago, we were practicing in Boston and it was 55 degrees," said BC guard Mark Bardwell. "Now we get here, it's 18 degrees, the ground's frozen. Whoever talked about the south, lied. But we don't mind. We're glad to be here."

"This is the way football used to be played," Bicknell said. "Out in the ice and cold. Now they have all these domes, and I'm not sure that's football. You have to be able to adjust to any type of weather or conditions."

After 15 minutes, he sent the team indoors.

"But that doesn't mean we have to practice in it," he added.

A boiler at the team hotel broke down, leaving some rooms without heat. Players woke up and found ice inside their windows. They never did practice outdoors. One day after practice, the team bus became stuck while trying to cross the icy railroad tracks.

When they investigated the Memphis nightlife, the Eagles ran into mostly Notre Dame players. The locals were staying home because of the weather and the holidays. "It's like the movie, 'The Day After,' " said a member of the BC entourage. "Nobody's around."

"We all went out Monday night," said a BC player, "and we ended up at a bar where there were a lot of Notre Dame players. The Notre Dame players were checking out Doug (Flutie) and then one of our guys goes to the men's room and he hears these Notre Dame guys talking. They're saying how Flutie looks like a little shrimp and they're not impressed by him and how they're going to tear him up in the game. Flutie hears all this and he gets really psyched—he wants to get at Notre Dame right away."

There was some worry about the grass field. The tarpaulin protecting it from the weather had been frozen. But it was removed and hay was spread along the icy grass outside of the field. The wet hay left the stadium smelling like manure. The wind chill factor was measured at zero degrees. Cold fans actually started fires in the stands to keep warm.

The Liberty Bowl could do nothing about the weather nor the silence of its local citizenry. The game itself was exciting.

BC scored on its first possession, but Waldron again slipped on the extra point. Bicknell decided that a soccer-style kicker would be ineffective on the frozen field. If BC's only option in some strange situation was to kick, then the kicker would have to be of the conventional, straight-on type. "Flutie," Bicknell said. He never had the chance to try.

Notre Dame blocked a punt to set up its go-ahead touchdown and followed Flutie's seventh straight incompletion (including a few dropped passes) with a 47-yard drive and a 19-6 lead.

Flutie passed 42 yards to Bob Biestek. Three plays later BC was at the Notre Dame 28. "Doug came up to the line and checked off," Gerard Phelan said. "He looked at me and he was smiling, nodding his head as if to say, 'You beat him to the inside, and it's yours.' I nodded back." Flutie threw the touchdown pass to Phelan, but the two-point conversion attempt failed. Notre Dame led, 19-12, at halftime.

BC held the Irish on fourth and one at the BC 15 early in the second half, and Flutie began a drive, pausing when he slid out of bounds and injured his left hip. Limping, he threw a three-yard touchdown to Scott Gieselman, but Gieselman dropped the two-point conversion. 19-18.

Neither team scored again, although Flutie took the Eagles from their 13 with 4:03 left, to the Notre Dame 35, where BC faced fourth and four in the final minute. Flutie knew the Irish would blitz all-out, "because they'd shown that defense four times this year and they came every time with seven or eight guys," he said. He slipped coming back from center, and while he was being sacked, got off a pass near Joe Giaquinto. Incomplete. Though BC lost, 19-18, it would be one of the most exciting bowl games of the year. Flutie was named Most Valuable Player of the game. And Gerry Faust kept his job for at least another season.

*　　　*　　　*

Flutie and Phelan had become roommates again during their sophomore year. "Gerard had become a different kid," said assistant coach Barry Gallup. "He started going out with the same girlfriend, the captain of the cheerleading team. He became more like Doug than ever." They were best friends, watching football games and competing to see who could recognize defenses first. The key game in Phelan's career may have been the Tangerine Bowl, when Flutie threw him five passes. "That really carried me into the next season," Phelan said. "It seemed like Doug got a lot of pleasure out of throwing the ball to me. He knew how much it meant to me. We'd sit around and talk and I'd say, 'If you get me on the post, you've got to get the ball to me.'"

They didn't room together on the road. "But we always end up in the same room, listening to music," Phelan said. "We like the same things."

Flutie was still dating Laurie Fortier, a secretary whom he had met when they were sophomores at Natick High School. He held the door open for her and walked her to class. Finally, he asked her out. Their first date was to a Red Sox game. Next was a high school baseball tournament, to see his brother Bill play. That night, Doug called and asked her to go steady, and she said yes.

Neither drank nor smoked. Flutie still came home most weekends. It seemed as if his parents were his true best friends. "Last Friday night, we're sitting here in the living room," Dick Flutie said in August before his son's senior year. "And Doug says, 'Let's go play golf.' Golf? It was night-time. But he drags us off to this little par-3 all-night golf course, and here we are, playing golf on a Friday night. It's great."

He thought of them during games. Dick and Joan had season tickets at the 20 yard line. "He looks for us," Joan Flutie said. "At BC, even when he wasn't playing, he'd look up, just to find us. Whenever anything good happens, he looks up and gives us one of these." Her thumb and index finger formed the 'OK' sign.

The Flutie's single-level white house in Natick was testimony to their relationship. Dick Flutie had filled file cabinets in the garage with his three sons' press clippings and programs. The walls in the den were covered with plaques, awards and team photos. Dick Flutie called the living room the "run-over room," for "the things we don't have room for in the other room."

"We bring a lot of people to the house," he said, "and everyone seems to ask why he doesn't have a big head. They can't seem to understand. See, this has always been a part of his life. He's always been a star, to us."

Dick and Joan were disappointed when they couldn't attend the Liberty Bowl. "The money ran out," Dick said. "There were some BC alumni who kindly said they would pay for tickets so our family could go, but I said, 'No, that's all right. We're just going to make sure we go to all the games next year.' "

He was a wedding photographer. "I must have worked at least eight weddings last summer," he said. "Just to make sure. We weren't going to miss any of the games." One of the weddings was Barry Gallup's.

And Doug followed the same rules. He would drive what the family drove, wear what the family provided. "People say, 'He dresses so well,' " Dick Flutie said. "I say, 'Look closer.' When he's dressed in a suit, he's wearing the same suit. When he's dressed in a sports jacket, he's wearing the same sports jacket. He has one suit. He has one sports jacket. Sometimes he'll borrow a sports jacket." He would borrow Gerard Phelan's. It was the one that didn't fit so well.

*　　　*　　　*

Trailing, 21-17, with less than a minute left in the 1984 BC Maroon and White spring game, Flutie drove his team 65 yards in four plays to the winning touchdown, scoring on a quarterback scramble around left end.

BC quarterback coach Tom Coughlin had already resigned to accept an assistant coaching position with the Philadelphia Eagles. He had been replaced by Sam Timer, for whom Bicknell had worked as a volunteer during that first coaching job at North Plainfield High School in New Jersey. BC linebacker coach Red Kelin had been an assistant on that North Plainfield staff, and BC defensive backs coach Pete Carmichael had been the quarterback.

After hearing that his brother Darren had signed with BC, and that Bicknell had turned down an interview to possibly coach the defending national champion

Miami Hurricanes at $200,000 a year, Flutie spent the summer before his senior season running a camp at a junior high school in Waltham, Massachusetts. He played infield for a Natick American Legion baseball team, and when he wasn't playing, he led cheers for Darren's Legion team. He played basketball, his favorite sport, in Worcester. He made a few speeches, warning students not to drink and drive.

He played a charity golf tournament with Bob Hope. He had his picture taken by *Sports Illustrated*, twice. He and 11 other athletes filmed TV messages one weekend at the Fiesta Bowl in Arizona, where he played golf with Miami quarterback Bernie Kosar; they tied, each shooting 44 in nine holes. He spent another weekend in Dallas with other Playboy All-Americas; he and Navy running back Napoleon McCallum late one night asked Dallas Cowboy running back Tony Dorsett for a ride back to the ranch (Flutie hadn't been drinking, of course). He was interviewed many times. He resumed eating at his favorite restaurant, a fast-food steakhouse. "He couldn't go there for a while because the manager kept trying to give Doug free dinners everytime he came in," Dick Flutie said.

Doug Flutie answered the phone during the summer, which he said he wanted to spend relaxing.

"It's tough," he said. "But you just have to learn to tell people 'no.' "

When the 1984 season finally began, most experts agreed Flutie was no longer the favorite to win the Heisman Trophy. Junior running back Bo Jackson, who had led Auburn to a No. 3 ranking at the end of the 1983 season, was expected to become the 13th consecutive non-quarterback to win the award.

12

Alabama

Flutie had it figured out.

"The Heisman is going to be determined by our won-lost record," he said before the 1984 season. "If we're 8-3 or 7-4, I won't win. If we're 11-0 or 10-1, I'll be in the running."

His teammates, including 16 returning starters, most from what Bicknell called "The Class Nobody Wanted," liked the part about going 11-0 . . . and the idea of a national championship.

"Anybody can come up and do it," said senior tight end Scott Gieselman. "A lot of it's luck, and we've been a Cinderella-type team in a lot of ways. Each year success builds on more success, and this year as a team we've been talking about it, about doing all the right things. If the breaks happen, realistically we could win every game on the schedule. It's not a cocky thing to say. It's a realistic goal."

It hadn't been realistic three years earlier.

"Obviously, I liked a lot of things about Jack," athletic director Bill Flynn said of his decision to hire Bicknell in 1981, "but I must say he has done a better job than I ever expected him to do."

The Eagles began with an easy 44-24 win against Western Carolina, which *Sports Illustrated* had ranked

No. 1 in the Division 1-AA preseason. Flutie had ended the first half by rolling right from the Western Carolina 18 and shot-putting a half-spiral into a group in the end zone. Troy Stradford leaped from the pack for a one-handed catch. The highlight film had begun.

The opener concluded, No. 18 BC prepared to go to Alabama, which was ranked No. 9 in the country. Two days before the nationally televised game, Alabama coach Ray Perkins, a former head coach of the New York Giants, was asked whether Flutie could play in the NFL.

"You aren't supposed to ask me that," Perkins said. But he answered it. "I don't think anybody will take a shot at him," Perkins said. "I think he would have a tough time in the NFL simply because the guys are a lot bigger in the NFL than they are in college. And I don't see the NFL utilizing the same kinds of schemes, roll-outs, that he uses in college.

"His only weakness is his height (though he had grown ¼-inch to stand 5-9¾). Some people don't think height means that much, but I'll guarantee you it does. It's just a big disadvantage.

"I think he would make a super, super Canadian (Football League) quarterback, because of his movement. He's got a real strong arm, he's very smart, and he's highly competitive."

"That's his opinion," Flutie said, "and he's entitled to it. He obviously knows what he's talking about."

The Eagles flew to Alabama on a Friday afternoon, checked in at the hotel for a couple of hours, then bused to Legion Field in Birmingham for a short workout. When they arrived, Dick Flutie couldn't find Doug.

"I think Doug and Gerard (Phelan) missed the bus," Dick Flutie said.

They and several others had misjudged the time change and caught a ride to the stadium. Flutie was embarrassed.

While ABC's Keith Jackson interviewed Flutie and smiling Dick Flutie took photos of his son, the Eagles looked about the empty stadium. More than 24 hours before the game, at least 30 motor homes were parked in the lot outside. The Goodyear blimp floated above them and the sign in the stands read, "BIRMINGHAM—FOOTBALL CAPITAL OF THE SOUTH."

"The first two years I was on the team, I think we were intimidated on these trips," said BC defensive tackle and tri-captain Scott Harrington. "Especially the older guys. They didn't want to play some of those games. You could see it."

The intimidation had been replaced by a sense of wonder.

"I came up in the elevator with (defensive backs coach) Pete Carmichael after we checked in," Bicknell said. "We grew up together, so we go way back. I just looked at him and said, 'Alabama. Pretty good for a couple of guys from North Plainfield, New Jersey, huh?' "

"So," Bicknell was asked, "how are you going to punish your tardy quarterback?"

"By making sure he sits next to me on the bus ride to the game tomorrow," he laughed.

*　　　*　　　*

He was on that bus. "But I didn't show up until the third quarter," Flutie complained. "I don't know what it was."

Alabama led, 24-14, at the half. Flutie had started nervously, and BC's defense hadn't stopped anything.

Then Alabama's Kerry Goode returned the second half opening kickoff 99 yards for a 31-14 lead.

"It got real quiet on the bench," Flutie said. "But there was still a lot of time."

Perkins obliged by replacing his starting quarterback, sophomore Mike Shula (son of Miami Dolphins' coach Don Shula), with freshman Vince Sutton. Sutton threw a pass that receiver Joe Smith fumbled at the BC 5—the key play of the game, since another Alabama touchdown would have finished BC. Flutie took BC inside the Alabama 20, but lost the ball on downs when he was called for passing over the line of scrimmage on fourth down. He was also hit hard on the play, suffering a bruised rotator cuff of his left shoulder that would force him to change his throwing motion.

Sutton then threw an out-pass from his 37 that BC safety Tony Thurman intercepted and returned to the 10. Flutie ran it in from five yards for 31-21, and soon afterward Kevin Snow kicked a field goal to narrow the gap to 31-24.

So Shula returned, but an enthused Eagles' defense held. On fourth and 1 at the Alabama 12, BC's Steve Strachan faked a dive into the line and Flutie threw to fullback Jim Browne for a touchdown to bring BC within a one-point conversion of tying it with 5:58 left.

"I said then that we were going for two (a two-point conversion)," Bicknell said. "(Offensive line coach) Mike Maser asked me, 'Are you sure?' And (quarterback coach) Sam Timer asked me, 'Are you sure?' And I said, 'We're going for two.'

"Then I said, 'Wait a minute. That's stupid.' "

Kevin Snow kicked the extra point. Tie game.

BC forced an Alabama punt, and at the Crimson Tide 42, Flutie changed the blocking assignments at the line. Stradford's hole off tackle was huge. Once in the open field, he had only one defensive back to beat, with a teammate to block him. His 42-yard touchdown run gave BC a 38-31 lead.

Tony Thurman's second interception gave Snow a chance at a game-clinching 29-yard field goal, which he missed. Then Alabama took the ball to the BC 28 where, with 53 seconds left, Sutton pitched right to tailback Paul Ott Carruth, who was readying to throw as teammate Joe Smith sprinted to the right corner of the end zone.

Thurman was near a hashmark. "I thought he (Carruth) was going to run the ball," Thurman said. Then he saw Smith. A pass! "I had to start breaking," said Thurman, shouting in the wild BC locker room. "I was just going to knock it down but then I knew I had to go for three."

His third interception of the game was a dive, maybe 15 feet, fingertip-first. Ironically, Thurman had been disappointed that he had dropped interceptions his previous year, and had returned to BC for a fifth year to improve his worth in the NFL draft. The best way to do that was by improving his catching, and he worked on it every day before practice. "I wouldn't have caught that ball last year," he said. He held onto the game-saving interception long enough to spike it, earning a penalty.

"I'm gonna bench Thurman for that unsportsman-like conduct penalty," Bicknell joked after the 38-31 win.

"Then you're gonna have to bench Flutie for missing the bus," answered defensive backs coach Pete Carmichael.

*　　　*　　　*

Flutie left Alabama with his left arm in a sling, but had an extra week to prepare for North Carolina at home. He hadn't forgotten the 56-14 loss of his freshman year, when tailback Kelvin Bryant had returned late in the blowout just to score another touchdown. Flutie rubbed down the game footballs the night before the game to gain an extra edge.

He didn't need it. While Carolina was rushing only three men and rarely pressuring Flutie, he was standing in the pocket, picking out receivers for a school-record six touchdown passes on national cable TV. On one he rolled out, jumped and threw over two Carolina defenders for a Troy Stradford touchdown catch. Another time he rolled left, looking as if he were going to run it in, before tossing a touchdown to Scott Gieselman as he would have a pitch-out, end-over-end.

The final score was 52-20, and Flutie had left early in the second half. "I wish I could have stayed in longer, like they did to us," he said.

"He could have dunked the ball if he wanted to," said Tar Heel coach Dick Crum.

Flutie had entered the season with more interceptions (46) than touchdown passes (45). Three victories into his senior year, he had thrown 12 touchdowns and just one interception. The Eagles had another two-week layoff (the BC-Miami game had been moved to Thanksgiving weekend to accommodate network TV), during which they climbed to No. 4 in the country. And Auburn's Bo Jackson was injured and would miss most of the season. Flutie was the Heisman Trophy favorite.

13

Decision

Both ABC and CBS followed Flutie during this two-week break to chronicle A Day In His Life. *People* magazine centered upon his relationship with Laurie Fortier. She told *People* they would probably be married after this year. "Guys were still asking me about the first game at Penn State," Flutie said. The interviews were making him irritable.

When the Boston College Eagles finally resumed against Temple October 13, it took a 51-yard touchdown pass to Gerard Phelan in an end zone crowd on the last play of the first half to give BC a 9-7 lead at intermission. The second half would be remembered for an inside reverse to Phelan, who pitched wide to Flutie, who was then thrown for a loss by one, two and then three Owls near the Temple bench. When one Owl wouldn't get off him, Flutie tried to shove him off. A baseball fight broke out (few punches were thrown), lasting until BC center Jack Bicknell, Jr. (the coach's son) lifted Flutie and carried him from the crowd.

The 24-10 victory against Temple carried the No. 4 Eagles (4-0) into a game at No. 20 West Virginia, the team responsible for BC's first losses of the last two years. But BC had won the Lambert-Meadowlands Trophy as the best team in the East in 1983, angering West

Virginia fans, who sent obscene letters to the Lambert voters. The secretary of state of West Virginia issued a proclamation that the Mountaineers were indeed "The Beast of the East," and he denounced the sports writers who had voted against West Virginia. Those who had voted *for* the Mountaineers received official proclamations naming them "ambassadors" of West Virginia.

Flutie termed the Lambert talk coming out of West Virginia as "really bush" and said he didn't want to finish his career without beating the Mountaineers. When he led BC to a 20-6 halftime lead, it appeared to be a goal he would accomplish.

In the West Virginia locker room, coach Don Nehlen had written '20' on a chalkboard. "We're going to hold them to this," Nehlen said.

They did, aided by officials who lost track of a BC down, forcing the Eagles to punt on what was actually third down. The Mountaineers slowly came back, running easily through BC the final 35 yards for a 21-20 lead. BC began from its 33 with 4:46 left, and in less than a minute Flutie brought the Eagles to the West Virginia 49. On fourth and four with 3:34 left, he rolled right, jumped and hit Troy Stradford, who knelt to make the first down catch at the Mountaineer 38; another 10 yards and BC's Kevin Snow could have kicked his second 45 yard field goal of the game. But Flutie was sacked by West Virginia's Fred Smalls and, on fourth and 24, Flutie lobbed a pass a few inches too far for tight end Scott Gieselman.

"I'll always be able to tell my grandchildren," Smalls said, "that I sacked Doug Flutie. I never thought it would happen to me."

The West Virginia fans threw bottles onto the field. A full can of beer knocked out an official working the first down chains. Bicknell told his players to wear their helmets on the sideline, and when the game was over, representatives of the 60,286 fans (the third-largest crowd ever at Mountaineer Field) took over the field.

The national championship? "I think it's out the window," Flutie said, slamming his locker shut.

*   *   *

Not so fast. The Eagles dropped to No. 11, and a win against Rutgers the following week put BC back into the Top 10, just in time for the rematch at Penn State.

The game marked BC's fourth network or cable TV appearance, and Flutie set an NCAA career total offense yards record everyone had known would be his. Unknown was that he would throw for 447 yards, setting an NCAA record for most career yards against one opponent (1,445 in 13 quarters vs. Penn State) and becoming the first player to gain 10,000 career yards in total offense.

Stradford had suffered a pulled hamstring against Rutgers, but backup tailback Ken Bell giant-slalomed to a 71-yard touchdown run and a first-half lead. In came Penn State backup quarterback Doug Strang, who would complete only 4 of 13 passes, but three for big plays. And he would strangle the Eagles for 52 scrambling yards; BC had already allowed Penn State's D.J. Dozier and Steve Smith more than 100 yards rushing each. Trailing, 29-17, in the fourth quarter, Flutie—who had suffered a slightly separated shoulder while leaping for a first down in the third quarter—asked Bicknell for permission to go into the hurry-up offense with 11:16 left as he had two years earlier; Bicknell allowed it this time. "The two-minute offense takes all the coaching and other stuff and throws it out the window," Flutie said. "It makes the players on the field react."

He reacted by creating 203 yards (200 by passing) and two touchdowns during the next seven minutes. Then he spent the last four agonizing minutes watching Penn State hold the ball to win, 37-30.

Again, fans who had been part of the largest crowd BC had ever played before (85,690 was also the fourth largest ever at Penn State's Beaver Stadium) celebrated on the field. "You know things have changed," Bicknell said, "when Penn State tears down the goalpost after beating BC."

As for the national championship, *now* it was finished.

"We can play for ourselves now," Flutie said.

And for a New Year's Day bowl bid. That hope still remained.

*   *   *

BC bought Flutie $750 shoulder-rib pads to protect his separated shoulder, allowing him to play the following week against Army. It was a good thing, because Army's wishbone ran through the Eagles, continually forcing BC to score to remain in control in the second half and win, 45-31. Had Flutie (19 of 29 for 311 yards and three TDs) not played well, BC probably would have lost. Meanwhile, he appeared to have captured another record, the career passing record, when he threw a touchdown pass to Darren, which would have been his brother's first touchdown. But a penalty nullified the play. "It would have been a nice touch," Darren said.

Bowl decision time was quickly approaching. BC had lost to two of three national powers on its schedule, its win coming at Alabama, which would suffer its first season without playing in a bowl game in 26 years. But the other teams were losing, too, and they didn't have the certain Heisman Trophy winner. Flutie's value was unsurpassed. The Cotton Bowl proclaimed BC its No. 1 choice, while the Sugar Bowl said it would take the Eagles if surprisingly undefeated South Carolina were to lose. "If BC just takes care of its knitting this next weekend, they'll be all right," said Cotton Bowl executive vice-president Jim Brock. BC's next opponent was Syracuse.

The Orangemen had been on a roll of sorts since beating BC in 1983. Syracuse had then upset West Virginia and pulled off the upset of 1984, beating No. 1 Nebraska. Syracuse brought a 6-4 record to Boston, hoping that a season-ending victory against BC would be worth a bowl bid.

The Cotton Bowl's Brock was opposed to that scenario. The one he liked had BC beating Syracuse. Then he hoped to check in with his committee and receive permission to offer the Eagles an unofficial bid after the game. However, it appeared half of his committee preferred to invite Nebraska, rather than BC—the Cotton Bowl didn't like the possibility that it could invite the Eagles and then watch BC lose at Miami, thus tarnishing the Cotton Bowl.

It appeared BC preferred the Cotton Bowl. Bicknell said privately he had grown up thinking the Cotton was the most prestigious bowl (although he added such a personal preference wouldn't be a major factor). BC athletic director Bill Flynn was telling friends that he would prefer the Cotton Bowl, too. Even Flutie seemed to like the Cotton Bowl, writing an autographed photo to Brock: "Hope to see you in Dallas."

When Brock arrived in Boston Thursday before the game, Flynn picked him up at the airport. When Sugar Bowl executive director Mickey Holmes arrived Friday, he rented a car. Someone gave him wrong directions and he got lost driving to BC. When he arrived, Flynn and Bicknell only spoke with him briefly. "I think they (the Cotton Bowl) have them (BC) locked," Holmes said in a hotel bar late Friday night. "I'm wondering why we are here."

Of course, BC still had to beat Syracuse. Flutie came out throwing for a 7-0 lead, but by halftime, BC trailed, 10-7. Trouble.

Here, the Eagles decided to learn from their mistakes of the previous year. After Syracuse had stopped Flutie the previous year, the Eagles realized they should have run the ball in key situations because those were the plays Syracuse was giving up; but the coaches had been afraid to take the ball out of Flutie's hands in the critical moments. They were still wary now, but they were also trailing by three points at halftime. They decided to run.

In the pressbox at halftime, Holmes was in a better mood. BC was suddenly showing more interest in his bowl. He felt a lot better about his chances, he said.

Flutie completed only 3 of 6 passes in the second half, but he ran a key third-and-22 quarterback draw for the first down near the Syracuse goal line. And Kelvin returned a punt for a touchdown for a 24-10 lead late in the game. But Syracuse came back within a minute, scoring on a bomb from midfield. The two-point conversion failed, but the Orangemen regained possession and began a drive in the final three minutes, trailing, 24-16. For BC, a tie would be as bad as a loss. But a win

would be perfect. They won when Tony Thurman solidi-
fied his place as the nation's leader in interceptions in
the final two minutes. "That ball," Thurman said after
his interception had saved the 24-16 win, "had January
1 written all over it."

So did the BC locker room. Representatives from
the Orange, Sugar and Cotton bowls waited in the BC
locker room after the game. South Carolina had been
upset at Navy. BC was now the No. 1 choice of the
Sugar and Cotton bowls. The Orange Bowl, stunned
because it had planned to offer a bid to South Carolina,
was unsure whom to invite. It could offer BC a bid, but
only upon the condition that the Eagles beat Miami the
following week.

The representatives stood near Flutie's locker.

He walked past them, putting his arm around Jim
Brock. "So what do you think?" Flutie said as they
walked out of the locker room together.

The Orange Bowl representatives watched, shaking
their heads: The Cotton Bowl.

The BC leaders walked into a towel closet at Sullivan Stadium, where the game had been played, and
shut the door behind them. The decision to play in any
of the three biggest bowl games rested with these men:
Rev. J. Donald Monan, S.J., president of BC; Jack
Bicknell, who had been a coach with an 18-35-1 record
at Maine four years earlier; Bill Flynn, who for many of
his first 25 years had been criticized for not taking BC to
even the most minor of bowls; and two tri-captains,
defensive end David Thomas and offensive tackle Mark
MacDonald, holdovers from the Ed Chlebek days
whom Bicknell had not even recruited. Bicknell had
tried to find Flutie and tri-captain Scott Harrington, but
they had already left.

"Fellas," Flynn told the two players, "it's wherever you want to go. What do you think?"

Flynn emerged from the room and walked toward Mickey Holmes of the Sugar Bowl. They walked together, talking, toward the bathroom. The Sugar Bowl?

"Well, that's it boys," said Brock, looking to be in need of an air sickness bag. "They're going to the Sugar Bowl."

Flynn returned to the closet, then quickly reappeared. He motioned reporters and TV news crews toward him for the announcement.

BC was going to play in the Cotton Bowl, win or lose against Miami next weekend.

"Why did you go into the bathroom with the man from the Sugar Bowl?" Flynn was asked later.

"I had to go to the bathroom," Flynn said. "I don't know why he was going there."

14

Miami

Someone has since called this the ultimate sandlot game, which is peculiar, considering neither principal player had ever seen a sandlot. Bernie Kosar instead appeared to be the ultimate chalk-lined grass-field quarterback, a model of park-league football and its maniacal, part-time coaches. This kid stood in the pocket, he ran the play the way it was supposed to be run, he was a coach on the field. Perfect spirals and quick releases weren't enough.

The perfect park-league player had to do as The Coach had planned to do, down to hitting the fourth receiver when the rest of the world would have thrown it away. That's how he won national championships. That's how he drove for the apparent winning touchdown in this final minute against Boston College. If there ever was an indication that our society is the true way, it lived in this kid. Bernie Kosar, future All-America and NFL star, because his coaches had loved him enough and cared enough for him to probably yell in his ear, every single day, for 10 wonderful years.

Watching this, the rain dripping from him, was Kosar's opposite.

"Let's call timeout," Flutie said.

"No," said Jack Bicknell, the Boston College fourth-year coach. "You just can't do that."

The funny thing, worth chuckling about—later—was the situation: BC 41, Miami 38, less than three minutes left. Penalties had pushed Miami quarterback Bernie Kosar into a third-and-21 pass from his end zone, where he was almost tackled for a safety. He completed a 20-yard pass. The Hurricanes gained five yards on fourth-and-one. Their drive for the winning touchdown began.

"Timeout?" Flutie said.

"No," Bicknell answered.

"I understood what he was trying to say," Bicknell would say later. "But suppose they botch a play . . . have to hurry a kick."

Flutie was saying that the Hurricanes—that Kosar—would force BC to score again. BC received the opening kickoff and Flutie completed his first 11 passes: 14-0, Eagles. Then Kosar passed successfully 11 consecutive times: 14-14. Flutie created new plays out of old, busted ones during the rest of the afternoon; Kosar, seven inches taller, remained in the pocket as ordered, never allowing a play to die. See? Neither would lose this game. Instead, one quarterback would only force the other into the position of having to win it. "This is what I can do," one would say. "Let's see you do better." The whole argument was that the quarterback who had the ball last would decide this game, provided he had enough time . . .

Too late. Kosar threw a wideout screen to Eddie Brown, who flung off a tackler and ran over BC All-America safety Tony Thurman. Thurman slid down Brown's leg and held his ankle. He was the bulldog chewing the postman's pants' leg. Brown tugged him to the 5, and Miami fullback Melvin Bratton scored from the 1.

From the sideline, Flutie nodded. Trailing, 45-41, his final turn would last 28 seconds with two timeouts. "All I was thinking was: 'They played well, they deserve it,' " he said. "All we have to do is get the ball to midfield. Then we're in range to just throw it into the end zone."

His teammates on defense weren't enthusiastic. "The only thought I had was that we had just lost the ballgame," said BC safety Dave Pereira.

BC tailback Troy Stradford grabbed dejected cornerback Vinnie Munn. "We're going to do it," Stradford said. "Don't worry. We're going to do it."

The Eagles downed Miami's kickoff in the end zone, facing 80 yards into a wind playing punch-bag with palm trees in the end zone behind them. "But it really wasn't all that bad to throw into," Flutie said. And the grass field held firm. "I've always felt the offense has the advantage on a wet day," Bicknell added.

"We can do it," Flutie said in the huddle. "No mistakes."

He passed 19 yards to Stradford. Penalty . . . Miami was guilty of holding. The clock stopped at 20 seconds. Flutie then sprinted a few yards toward Scott Gieselman before throwing to him near the left, Miami sideline. Gieselman turned and ran out at the Hurricane 48.

Stradford jogged to the huddle. "Doug," he said, "we've got to go for 'flood tip.' "

"OK," Flutie said.

But he had another plan first. However, he overthrew tight end Peter Caspariello near the Miami 25.

"That would have been a big play," Flutie said. He looked at the scoreboard. Six seconds remained.

A messenger was sent to the huddle with the play, but Flutie waved him back. "I knew what they wanted to call," he said, "and I wanted to run it with the players we had on the field." The play was "55 Flood Tip." BC practiced it every Thursday, aligning three receivers on the right side with orders to sprint downfield. Flutie would wait until they were near the goal line. "Then you throw," he said, "and pray. It's a 50-50 chance your guy will come up with it."

Actually, the probability was that no one would catch it. But his flood-tip stats weren't bad. Six games earlier, he had completed a 51-yarder to receiver Gerard Phelan, ending the first half with a touchdown against Temple; another had gone through teammate Brian Brennan's hands, incomplete, in the first half against Notre Dame in the 1983 Liberty Bowl. In neither case had the ball been tipped. "That's the way it's supposed to go," Bicknell said. "But if it hits you in the chest, you catch it."

The Hurricanes expected it. Three linemen were ordered to rush Flutie, and a linebacker was told to remain in front of him, in case he tried to run for the touchdown. Two defensive backs crouched within 10 yards of right-side receivers Stradford and Kelvin Martin; two others waited some 20 yards from middleman Phelan. "This is something you work on all the time," said Miami defensive coordinator Bill Trout. "The safety (Darrell Fullington) is supposed to be deeper than their deepest receiver. We're jamming people up front, and he's supposed to be the centerfielder."

Kosar and teammates were celebrating, but Bratton, a freshman who had received and rushed for 218 yards and four touchdowns in his first start, felt uneasy. "This game isn't over," he told substitute receiver Kenny Oliver. "There's something wrong, Kenny, something wrong. Something weird might happen."

In the huddle, Flutie told Caspariello to sprint into the left side of the end zone. "I might come back to you," he said.

The game was out of Bicknell's hands. "I'm thinking about what I'm gonna say to the kids after the loss," he said. "I mean, you always say you're never out of it, but really . . ."

Doug took the snap.

Senior fullback Steve Strachan ran past Flutie, through the line toward the right end zone. "I'm supposed to stay back there to pick up anyone who slips off," Strachan said. "But on the last play, nobody's going to slip off. I figured I'd get down there because we could use as many people as possible."

Flutie dropped straight back five yards until Miami left tackle Jerome Brown tripped at Flutie's feet. No problem: His receivers needed the time Flutie spent half-circling to his right, around Brown and behind the BC 40 yard line. He approached the 38 like a javelin thrower, releasing a low-trajectory pass with one second left. "I know I can throw it 75 yards," he said. "I was afraid of sailing it out of the end zone."

His receivers weren't yet in the end zone, but they weren't being held, either.

"They were letting me get downfield," Strachan said.

"They weren't going after me at all," added Phelan who, as the man ordered to tip the ball to a teammate, was the designated key to the play. When he turned near the 10 yard line and saw Flutie throwing, he ran for the goal line.

"I was watching from the sideline, and Kelvin beat his man," said BC's Pereira. "But I saw Troy get held up. Now we only had two guys down there."

"To tell you the truth," said Miami linebacker George Mira, Jr., who was on the sideline, "I had this funny feeling for an instant that someone was going to catch it. But you always feel that way for an instant. Then you think, 'No way.' "

"When the ball was halfway there," said Miami's Trout, "I felt we were going to make the play."

Here, Fullington disregarded his assignment. He didn't believe Flutie could throw into the end zone, so he moved to inside the 5-yard line, allowing Phelan to get two yards behind him.

Strachan approached them. "I was trying to look for the ball," he said, "and I didn't think it was catchable for me. I had a guy on me and I didn't want to create a situation where I would ruin a teammate's chance to catch it, so we both fell and I just watched it."

Fullington had turned, facing Flutie with both hands above his head. "He must have figured, 'I've got this one; I'm going to pick it off,' " Phelan said.

Fullington suddenly lunged with one arm for the ball he had misjudged. At the height of his leap, teammate Tolbert Bain jumped into him.

Stradford said Fullington tipped the pass. "If he did," said Phelan, "it didn't alter the flight of it much."

Looking over his right shoulder, he turned toward the ball. His left foot was on the goal line when the ball struck the *20* on his uniform. "I landed," he said, "and I saw that there was writing on the ground underneath me. I jumped up fast to show the referee I had the ball."

He kept it. The ball is in his bedroom now.

"I thought I saw the ball hit the ground," said BC offensive tackle Mark MacDonald. "I turned to shake the hand of the guy I'd been playing against, to congratulate him. Then I saw him just slump over."

"I thought the ball was incomplete," Flutie said. "I saw the ref's arm go up but I didn't believe him. Then I looked on the Miami sideline and they were all just standing there."

And the scoreboard read BC 47, Miami 45, 0:00.

"I don't think I had a thought," Trout said. "Just nothing. When he made that catch, everything just stopped. Everyone just stopped. Everything just froze. Everyone just froze."

"I never saw him catch it," Bicknell said. "I never saw anything. Our guys were running with their hands up and it took me a while to realize what had happened. So if the camera was on me, I was probably standing looking like a big dope because I didn't know what had happened.

"I ran across the field to shake (Miami coach) Jimmy Johnson's hand. His face . . . his face was the way I suppose my face would have been if something like that had happened to me. I actually felt sorry for him."

Teammates had jumped Phelan when Flutie realized what had happened. He jumped into teammates' arms while working his way downfield. "I was under control," he said. "It's funny, but while it all was taking place I was pretty good. I wasn't very emotional at all. It was after it all happened, as I ran down the field, that I got emotional."

Realizing he had completed 2 of 4 flood-tip passes, he added. "See? I told you it was a 50-50 chance."

"I laughed," said Miami's Bratton, who had scored the "winning" touchdown 28 seconds earlier. "I had to laugh. It was just so crazy, so strange, what else could you do?"

"I was sitting in the locker room afterward," said BC safety Pereira, "and I was thinking how unbelievable the whole situation had been. And then I heard the other guys start yelling about the Lambert Trophy and that we're going to go up in the ratings and the Cotton Bowl and all the things this victory gave us, and I'd never even thought of those things. If I look back on my career, if I never play another down, I'll never be able to believe how unbelievable, how incredible, these last three years have been."

Offensive guard Mark Bardwell sat and shook for a half hour.

"That wasn't Gerard Phelan who caught that ball," Mark MacDonald said. "God caught that ball."

"No," lineman Jim Ostrowski said softly. "God threw it."

15

Heisman!

Moments after The Play, his teammates dumped a bucket of water over his head in the Orange Bowl visitors' lockerroom, the doors were opened, and the week began. Hundreds of fans waited for BC's plane to arrive late Friday night. ABC wanted to interview Flutie live Saturday; too tired, Flutie asked Gerard Phelan to make the appearance instead. CBS interviewed Flutie Sunday. He attended a Cotton Bowl pep rally Monday, then was interviewed for four hours. After announcing the BC-Miami game, Brent Musburger said he was staying at CBS because Doug Flutie had reminded him how exciting his job was. An Internal Revenue Service spokesman at a dinner in Boston said he was looking forward to accepting Doug Flutie's 1985 returns.

Enough! Jack Bicknell said. He shut Flutie off from the media.

The hysteria of the week didn't stop. Flutie was due to receive the Heisman Trophy (he refused to admit he was assured of winning it) on December 1, eight days after the BC-Miami game and only four hours after his final regular season game, at Holy Cross. David Letterman wanted Flutie on his show. ABC news and ABC sports wanted him. So did CBS sports. He was on the cover of *Sports Illustrated* again. The Tonight Show called. Phones seemed to ring constantly in Reid Oslin's

BC Sports Publicity office. Oslin's feeling was that he could unplug them and they would still ring.

"When does Johnny Carson want Doug?" Olsin was asked.

"I don't know," he said, head in hands. "I haven't returned the call yet."

People wanted as much Doug as they could get.

"It was The Pass that did it," Bicknell said. "It was like somebody came and threw a match on the whole thing."

"It's not just the interviews," Flutie said, sitting in the Eagles Lounge at BC's Roberts Center the Friday afternoon before his final regular season game and the Heisman night. "It's the combination of interviews and autographs. I love signing autographs for kids. Kids are great. It's when the parents come up to you and say they need an autograph for each of their three kids and all of their nephews. And there are some of these kids who want extra autographs. You're always hearing a kid walk away, saying, 'Boy, this is my fifth one.' "

He said he had one more goal. He wasn't sure if he wanted to announce it.

"I want to throw a touchdown pass to Darren [his brother]," Flutie said. "I haven't thrown one to him all year. I hope it happens. It will happen. Everything else has happened to me. This will, too."

Flutie appeared relaxed, rested. He was interrupted by a visitor. It was ABC announcer Jack Whitaker, who had done the first national TV story on Flutie.

"I guess it's been, what, a good two years since we talked," Whitaker said.

"It sure has," Flutie said.

They walked across the street to Alumni Stadium where the TV crew waited. Some 30 kids were playing catch on the field. An ABC employee told them they could sit in the stands and watch the interview if they remained quiet. They listened to Whitaker ask Flutie about his height and the possibilities of pro football. For perhaps the 500th time of the season, he said all he wanted was a chance to play.

Interview completed, the kids surrounded Flutie. He signed every autograph. "Wow," a kid said, looking at his. "This is my fourth one."

"See?" Flutie said. "Four autographs. What do you need four autographs for?"

The kids jumped over the railing and onto the field. Flutie threw one a pass. Then he sent them all long, threw again and walked away before it landed, smiling.

*　　　*　　　*

The BC Eagles spent the night before the game at a hotel, as usual. "We were watching a TV special about BC," said junior tailback Troy Stradford, "and I said, 'Just think, Doug. Tomorrow night you're going to go to New York and pick up the Heisman Trophy.' He didn't even look at me. He never knew if they were going to call out his name. But I was sure the whole time he was going to get it."

The next day, Division 1-AA Holy Cross—BC's chief rival since 1896—blitzed Flutie in the first half. His receivers dropped three passes, Flutie threw two interceptions and BC led only 17-10 at halftime. "We really weren't expecting them to blitz that much," said BC offensive backs coach Michael Godbolt. "They sold their souls to try to pressure Doug."

They lost. BC scored touchdowns on four of its first five possessions in the third quarter while Flutie returned to normal, completing 4 of 5 for 116 yards and two touchdowns. One, of course, was a pass to his brother Darren in the right corner. Doug Flutie jogged off the field with 12:40 left in the game, on third and 6, a passing down.

Teammates carried Bicknell and Flutie off of the field. "Doug was all embarrassed," said BC strong safety Dave Pereira. "He kept saying, 'Let me down, let me down.' "

At least 100 fans were crowded in the small patch of blacktop outside the visitors lockerroom at Holy Cross' Fitton Field. Police surrounded Flutie and pushed their way through the crowd. Inside, he was interviewed quickly by sports publicity assistant John Conceison, congratulated by teammates and then escorted again to a van.

The entourage was driven to Worcester Airport: the Flutie family and Doug's girlfriend, Laurie Fortier, Jack and Lois Bicknell, Barry Gallup, quarterback coach Sam Timer, Mr. and Mrs. Bill Flynn, BC president Rev. J. Donald Monan, S.J., Tom Lamb (Flutie's coach at Natick High School), and BC sports publicist Reid Oslin. Another crowd was waiting for Flutie. He walked up the stairs of the private plane, turned and waved, and was gone.

At 5 p.m. that day Flutie and his girlfriend, Laurie Fortier, approached the lights of Manhattan in a helicopter. "I'll tell you what," the pilot said. "I'm supposed to take you right over to the Downtown Athletic Club, but we have a little time. Let me see what we can do."

The pilot radioed to the control tower at LaGuardia Airport. Would it be possible to take Doug Flutie for a fast tour of the city?

"For Doug Flutie," the voice of the radio said, "you can go anywhere you want."

The helicopter finally landed and they took a limousine to the club. An hour later, he sat in the front row of the audience with the other Heisman candidates, Ohio State running back Keith Byars and Miami quarterback Bernie Kosar, and waited. The Heisman Trophy winner was to be announced at the end of an hour-long nationally televised special. The first 50 minutes were spent watching a Bud Greenspan film about the Heisman. Each minute was as an hour.

"He's had his heart broken before," explained Joan Flutie, Doug's mother. "There have been other trophies he was told he was going to receive, and they were given to someone else."

When was that?

"Midget football," she said. "There was one year he was supposed to win all the trophies and he didn't win one. It broke his heart."

The special finished. Downtown Athletic Club officials took turns introducing each other at the podium. "I tried to put it out of my mind, out of my mind until we played Holy Cross," Bicknell said. "Then we came down here and I was fine, and then, just sitting in that room, waiting for the announcement, I started to get tense. I wanted him to win it so badly."

In Chestnut Hill, Massachusetts, the dark road encircling the BC campus was empty. Troy Stradford, so sure his teammate would win, sat before a television set with friends.

"Hey, Troy," one said, "why do you have your fingers crossed?"

"I don't know," Stradford said.

At approximately 7:55 p.m., a spokesman for the Heisman Trophy announced that the winner was from "Boston College . . ."

That was all it took. The screams of students inside dormitories could be heard in the streets.

In New York, Dick Flutie turned to his wife and cried. His son, Doug, shook hands with the two other candidates, straightened his blazer and walked to the podium.

"When you're all alone, all by yourself, you wonder how it all happened," Doug Flutie said. "You don't know. You're just playing hard, trying to win games, trying to do what you're supposed to do, and suddenly it's all blown up, out of proportion."

People walked by, congratulating him. Everyone who knew him was being interviewed. It was all so . . . incredible? One scholarship offer . . . fourth-string quarterback . . . "Flutie, see what you can do." . . . five-foot-nine and three-quarters . . . and now the Heisman Trophy.

Dick Flutie took in all that surrounded him.

"The little kid," the father said, almost to himself. "The little kid."

One hundred students were waiting at his dorm when Flutie returned to Chestnut Hill at midnight. His roommates had a cake waiting for him. They relaxed, and then Dick and Joan drove Doug home, to Natick.

He appeared at halftime of a BC basketball game and received a standing ovation. Boston Mayor Raymond L. Flynn invited him to turn on the Christmas lights at the Common. Then he flew to New York.

He appeared in a parade. He taught New York Mayor Ed Koch how to hold a football (he couldn't teach Koch how to throw one). He met President Reagan for the second time. He was flown to Dallas as a Kodak All-American the following weekend. After eight days on the road, he was exhausted.

Practices began for the Cotton Bowl. Someone stole Doug's helmet. Doug asked that it be returned. It was returned. The story was front page news in the Sunday *Boston Herald*. Everyone wanted Doug. Doug wanted quiet. No quiet. Barry Gallup named his newborn son Darren Douglas Gallup. He was no longer Flutie. He was just Doug.

On Christmas morning, Doug asked Laurie Fortier to marry him. She accepted.

On December 26, he flew to Dallas and the Cotton Bowl.

"You never think you have to worry about people looking for autographs from a college kid," Bicknell said. "Well, I think everyone in Boston received an autographed picture of Doug Flutie for Christmas. It's unbelievable. The kid signed so many he had a blister on his finger. The team autographed 78 footballs."

"Have you seen the Doug Flutie earrings?" asked Joan Flutie. "Our son Bill's wife, Donna, has them. It's his signature. Doug Flutie. I think they look horrible."

The Pilot, the Boston Archdiocesan newspaper, reported how Doug had to leave Mass early because of the autographs. His father had to buy an answering machine. "We flew Eastern today, OK?" said Reid Oslin the day BC arrived at the Cotton Bowl. "Everything was fine, except our gate was next to the gate for the shuttle from New York. Just before we were going on the plane, the shuttle arrived and there it was. The people spotted him and we needed the state troopers just to get him out of there."

"It really got to me about a week ago," Doug said in Dallas. "There's always one more person who only needs you to do one more thing and, well, you're the one who has to do it. I've had an opportunity to see a lot of people and I've begun to see through some of them now. I've seen how a lot of them are trying to get something from you. I've become older, I guess. Or more mature. It had to happen sometime, I suppose. Life has changed, but I don't think it has changed for the better."

But he said he was rested, now, and prepared for his final game. No. 8 Boston College (9-2) vs. Houston (7-4) on New Year's Day.

*   *   *

Some 17,000 Bostonians had arrived in Dallas for the game. "The last home game before Doug Flutie first played," said Reid Oslin, "Boston College sold 16,200 tickets (at 32,000-seat Alumni Stadium). For a home game. Imagine that. Seventeen thousand people flying down now." A pep rally was held in the huge lobby of the BC team hotel on New Year's Eve. Thousands attended. Two trumpeteers played "For Boston" perhaps seven times. Then the band and cheerleaders arrived and took over. In the lockerroom before the game, Flutie and the other seniors joked about how "this is the last time" they would have their ankles taped. It was the last time they would play on the same team.

"I didn't even give a speech before the game," Bicknell said. "I know I'm supposed to give a speech about seniors and four years and all the rest. I didn't do anything. I'm an emotional person. If I thought about all the things that happened in these four years, I would have been crying by the time the second sentence was finished. I didn't want the kids to see me like that."

It was 32 degrees with 17 miles per hour winds and the artificial turf field was slippery. Flutie wore "rain" shoes that Bicknell had borrowed from his friend, Southern Methodist coach Bobby Collins. Flutie's first pass set one tone of the game—Gerard Phelan slipped trying to come back for the ball.

Another early pass set another tone. Flutie looped a bomb over late-arriving Houston cornerback Greg Purcell for a 67-yard touchdown that made it 7-0. Though the wind and field would affect Flutie all day, the Cougars had to remain wary of big plays because the conditions weren't going to stop Flutie from going for quick scores.

Flutie threw eight yards to Troy Stradford for 14-0 and, after Houston's Earl Allen had returned a kickoff 98 yards for a touchdown, Flutie struck again. While fullback Steve Strachan faked a dive play on third and one at the Houston 13, Flutie dropped back and hit Phelan over the middle for his third touchdown, tying a Cotton Bowl record for TD passes. He had played only 21 minutes and 19 seconds.

BC was controlling every phase of the game. Stradford ran for more than 100 yards in the first half. The Eagles had not allowed the Houston offense past the BC 39 yard line and Cougar quarterback Gerald Landry missed his first 10 passes. But a BC linebacker erred, calling for a defensive formation that BC hadn't practiced, and it allowed Houston tight end Carl Hilton to gain 38 yards, leading to a quick Houston touchdown at the end of the first half and a 31-14 BC lead at halftime. "That was a big score for them," Flutie said.

Flutie could complete only 2 of 13 for 14 yards in the second half. Late in the third quarter, less than a minute after Houston had scored to come within 10 points, Flutie one-handed a high shotgun snap. He was supposed to run a naked bootleg left, but Cougars were waiting for him. Quickly he noticed tight end Scott Gieselman open and threw. But Flutie hadn't had a good grip on the ball, and it fluttered in the wind and was intercepted by Houston's Audrey McMillian, who returned it for a touchdown. 31-28.

"Doug looked a little dull in the eyes," Bicknell said. "That was because he was frustrated. He knows he's supposed to be great every game and it bugs him when he isn't."

On the sideline, Flutie and the offense held a quick meeting. "Guys, I know we can move the ball," Flutie said. "Let's go out and do it."

They ran it. Nine straight times. Steve Strachan, voted offensive player of the game, scored the touchdown that made it 38-28. Stradford would score again for the 45-28 final score, the first Boston College bowl win since Frank Leahy had coached the Eagles to an undefeated 1940-41 season and a Sugar Bowl victory.

Jack Bicknell was carried off the field. Mark Bardwell, the "No. 1 recruit" who had started on the BC offensive line the last two years, and Gerard Phelan, Flutie's best receiver and best friend, grabbed Flutie's arms and sprinted him to a CBS postgame interview, and then to the lockerroom. It was not a melancholy scene. "The music was blasting and people were dancing," said BC strong safety Dave Pereira, who had also played his last game. Bicknell made no speech.

It wasn't necessary. In a strange way, Flutie had done his teammates the ultimate honor. He had not dominated his final game—there had been few successful scrambles, no wonderful diving passes. Instead, he had played well early, putting BC in control. From then the job of winning the game was shared by his teammates. Houston's offense had scored only 14 points.

BC's running game gained 353 yards, second-most in Cotton Bowl history, most ever under Jack Bicknell. Flutie's claim that he was not totally responsible for BC's success had been proven out. This team that would finish No. 5 in the country had not been all Flutie. He had just been the leader of The Class Nobody Wanted.

"Sure, I would have liked people to have walked away shaking their heads about how great Doug Flutie is," Doug Flutie said an hour after his final game. "Am I satisfied? Not based on my personal performance, no. With the game itself, yes. If I had a choice between this and the Heisman, I wanted this. I'm happiest for this."

Appendix: Stats

Doug Flutie Awards

1984

- Heisman Trophy winner
- Maxwell Club Trophy winner
- Player of the Year, United Press International and The Sporting News
- First team All-America Associated Press, United Press International, Kodak (American College Football Coach's Association), Walter Camp Foundation, The Sporting News and Football Writers Association of America
- Playboy preseason All-America
- ECAC Player of the Year Award
- Gold Helmet Award (New England Football Writers Association)
- O'Melia Award vs. Holy Cross
- George Bulger Lowe Award (Gridiron Club of Boston)
- National Football Foundation post-graduate scholarship
- Rhodes Scholarship nominee

1983

- Third place, Heisman Trophy
- ECAC Player of the Week vs. Army
- Liberty Bowl Most Valuable Player
- NBC Sportsman of the Week vs. Clemson
- UPI All-America Second Team

1982

- Chevrolet Most Valuable Player in network TV games vs. Texas A&M and Clemson
- Tangerine Bowl Outstanding Offensive Player

1981

- ECAC Co-Rookie of the Year
- O'Melia Award winner vs. Holy Cross

Doug Flutie's NCAA Division 1-A Records

Total offense

- most yards gained, career: 11,317
- most seasons gaining 3000 yards or more: Two, 1982 and 1984 (shared with Steve Young, Brigham Young 1982-83; Tony Eason, Illinois 1981-82; Jim McMahon, Brigham Young 1980-81)
- most seasons gaining 2500 yards or more: Three, 1982-84 (Randall Cunningham, Nevada-Las Vegas 1982-84; John Elway, Stanford 1980-82)
- most yards gained against one opponent, career: 1445 vs. Penn State, 1981-84
- most yards gained per game against one opponent (minimum four games): 361.3 vs. Penn State, 1981-84
- most yards gained by two opposing players, one game: 953, Flutie and Bernie Kosar, Miami (1984—Flutie 517, Kosar 436)

Passing

- most yards gained, career: 10,579
- most yards gained passing, by two opposing Division 1-A players, one game: 919, Flutie (472) and Bernie Kosar, Miami (447), 1984
- most yards gained per pass completion, career (minimum 400 completions): 15.6 (677 completions for 10,579 yards)

The road to the '84 trophy

GAME 1: NO. 19 BC 44, WESTERN CAROLINA 24
September 1, Alumni Stadium (32,000 Sellout)

The last 4000 tickets were sold on game day, and the first of four Alumni sellout crowds saw Flutie play only one series into the third quarter. BC scored TDs on five of its first eight possessions. BC tried to develop a running game early, before Flutie took over. He scrambled out of a third-and-31, throwing crossfield to Scott Gieselman for a first down at the WC 1; he picked up a fumbled handoff and ran 13 yards; and with 1:01 left in the first half, he drove BC from its 26 to the WC 18. In the final five seconds, he rolled right and—a yard from the right sideline, with three Catamounts chasing him—shot-putted a half-spiral into a group, from which Troy Stradford leaped and one-handed the ball for the TD.

GAME 1 STATS

Score	Comp.	Att.	Yds.	Pct.	Int.	TD BC passes	BC rush.	Flutie att./rush	Sacks /yds.	BC fumb.	Score at half
44-24	22	31	330	.710	1	4	258	1/12	0/0	0	34-7

GAME 2: NO. 18 BC 38, NO. 9 ALABAMA 31
September 8, Legion Field (67,821), National TV, Prime Time

The greatest comeback (so far) led to ABC commentator Frank Broyles' emergence as Flutie's national spokesman. Alabama tailback Kerry Goode rushed through the Eagles. Then Goode returned the second-half kickoff 99 yards for a 31-14 lead. The game turned when Alabama coach Ray Perkins inexplicably replaced starting QB Mike Shula with freshman Vince Sutton, who threw a pass that was fumbled and recovered at the BC 5. Flutie—who had scrambled circles around Alabama pass-rushing linemen, sending them crashing into each other as he completed a fourth-and-goal first-half TD pass to Steve Strachan—brought BC back, helped by Troy Stradford's 43-yard winning TD with 3:26 left. Goode suffered torn knee ligaments, and BC stopped Alabama until its final drive; the Tide tried a halfback-option with 45 seconds left, and

BC safety Tony Thurman dived into the end zone for his third interception of the night.

GAME 2 STATS

Score	Comp.	Att.	Yds.	Pct.	Int.	TD passes	BC rush.	Flutie att./rush	Sacks /yds.	BC fumb.	Score at half
38-31	19	38	254	.500	0	2	152	11-21	2-20	1	14-24

GAME 3: NO. 10 BC 52, NORTH CAROLINA 20
September 22, Sullivan Stadium (44,671), National Cable TV

A second straight exciting national TV performance, combined with injuries to running backs Bo Jackson of Auburn and Napoleon McCallum of Navy, made Flutie the Heisman favorite. But while Game 2 had featured Flutie vs. The South, this one was Everything You Wanted To Know About Flutie. "Probably Doug's best all-around game," said BC coach Jack Bicknell. Flutie took control of the Heisman with a school-record six touchdowns. North Carolina chose to drop eight defenders into pass coverage, leaving Flutie too much time to find an open receiver—his first 20 passes hit BC receivers. Yet the few times the Tar Heels pressured Flutie led to the most exciting plays. Once, he spun out of All-America linebacker Micah Moon's sack. His third touchdown pass was off a rollout—he skip-jumped to throw over a couple of North Carolina's linemen, their arms outstretched (too short?), to throw a 14-yarder to Troy Stradford. He rolled left and chest-passed 4 yards for his fourth TD.

GAME 3 STATS

Score	Comp.	Att.	Yds.	Pct.	Int.	TD passes	BC rush.	Flutie att./rush	Sacks /yds.	BC fumb.	Score at half
52-20	28	38	354	.737	0	6	258	2/33	0/0	0	28-0

GAME 4: NO. 4 BC 24, TEMPLE 10
October 13, Alumni Stadium (32,000 Sellout)

BC had climbed in the polls while others lost during BC's 20-day layoff, but the Eagles lost the momentum of two big wins. Probably Flutie's worst game (three interceptions) of the season produced another highlight: On fourth and 11, with seven seconds left in the first half, he threw some 60 yards into a nine-man crowd at the goal line. Gerard Phelan slid in front of an Owl, stole it from him, looked down and saw his feet were an inch inside the goal line. BC held Temple to a field goal in the second half, which will be remembered for an inside reverse to Phelan, who pitched wide to Flutie, who was thrown for a loss at the Temple bench and began a fight by trying to push an Owl off him. "The one thing we're going to do is protect Doug Flutie," said fullback Steve Strachan.

GAME 4 STATS

Score	Comp.	Att.	Yds.	Pct.	Int.	TD passes	BC rush.	Flutie att./rush	Sacks /yds.	BC fumb.	Score at half
24-10	17	33	257	.515	3	1	140	7/-2	3/-17	1	9-7

GAME 5: NO. 20 WEST VIRGINIA 21, NO. 4 BC 20
October 20, Mountaineer Field (60,286, Third Largest Ever),
National TV

Trailing, 20-6 at halftime, West Virginia coach Don Nehlen wrote *20* on a chalkboard in the locker room. "We're going to hold them to this," he announced. In the second half, the Eagles suffered a bad field position, gained an average of 1 yard on first down and ran for minus-28 yards in the half, allowing the Mountaineers to guess BC would pass. So the Eagles gained only 105 yards overall in the half. The last time the Mountaineers had the ball, they drove 80 yards on Kevin White possession passes and John Gay's four runs for the final 35 yards. BC then began from its 33 with 4:46 left, needing only a field goal to win. In less than a minute, Flutie had passed BC to the West Virginia 49. On fourth and 4 with 3:34 left, he rolled right, jumped and hit Troy Stradford for a first down at the 38; another 11 yards, and Kevin Snow (who had kicked 41- and 45-yarders) could try a 45-yard field goal. But Flutie was sacked for 11 yards, a pass to Stradford lost 3 more, another was incomplete, and a fourth-and-24 lob was thrown a few inches too far for Scott Gieselman at the 18.

GAME 5 STATS

Score	Comp.	Att.	Yds.	Pct.	Int.	TD passes	BC rush.	Flutie att./rush	Sacks /yds.	BC fumb.	Score at half
20-21	21	42	299	.500	0	1	19	5/-33	3/-38	1	20-6

GAME 6: NO. 11 BC 35, RUTGERS 23
October 27, Alumni Stadium (32,000 Sellout), Regional TV

Rutgers kept Flutie off the field; the Scarlet Knights held the ball for 34:50 and 102 plays and gained 20 yards on a play only twice. That was the difference. Flutie's first two TDs were against blitzes; he completed 14 of 20 for 243 yards and 3 TDs in the first half. Ken Bell returned the second-half opening kickoff 92 yards to Rutgers' 5, and Flutie scored immediately on an option keep (the second of four one-play series for BC) for a 28-10 lead. Rutgers held the ball for 20:58 of the second half. "It was frustrating," said Flutie. "I hate it." The game came down to Rutgers QB Rusty Hochberg, trailing by 12 points, throwing on fourth-and-goal in the final three minutes. Safety Dave Pereira knocked the ball to Tony Thurman, but his interception didn't count because none of the officials saw it.

GAME 6 STATS

Score	Comp.	Att.	Yds.	Pct.	Int.	TD passes	BC rush.	Flutie att./rush	Sacks /yds.	BC fumb.	Score at half
35-23	21	30	318	.700	2	3	121	5/25	0/0	2	21-10

GAME 7: PENN STATE 37, NO. 9 BC 30
November 3, Beaver Stadium (85,690, Fourth Largest Ever), Regional TV

Flutie set NCAA records for most career offensive yards (10,003) and most career yards gained against one opponent (1445 in 13 quarters vs. Penn State). Ken Bell's 71-yard TD run gave BC a first-half lead, but Penn State backup QB Doug Strang scrambled for 52 yards. Strang completed only 4 of 13 passes, but three were for big plays. Penn State scored quickly in the second half for a 23-17 lead that put the Nittany Lions in control. Their backfield of D.J. Dozier (21 rushes for 143 yards) and Steve Smith (23 for 126) drove through the Eagles defense, keeping the ball and building a 29-17 lead early in the fourth quarter. Flutie, who had suffered a minor separation of his left shoulder while leaping for a first down in the third quarter, suggested going to a hurry-up offense with 11:16 left: In the following three possessions during the next seven minutes, he created 203 yards (throwing for 200) and two touchdowns. But Strang scrambled for a first down in the final two minutes, ending any BC hopes of a national championship.

GAME 7 STATS

Score	Comp.	Att.	Yds.	Pct.	Int.	TD passes	BC rush.	Flutie att./rush	Sacks /yds.	BC fumb.	Score at half
30-37	29	53	447	.547	2	1	113	10/-26	4/-52	3	17-17

GAME 8: NO. 16 BC 45, ARMY 31
November 10, Alumni Stadium (32,000 Sellout), Regional TV

He was under a strange kind of pressure throughout his final game at Alumni Stadium, and it had nothing to do with the $750 pads protecting his injured shoulder. After throwing for two touchdowns and watching Kelvin Martin return a punt 45 yards for BC's fourth unanswered TD and a 28-7 lead, surprising Army initiated the first two-minute wishbone. The Cadets drove 68 yards in 1:25 at the end of the half to make it 28-14 at halftime. Flutie began the second half with four straight completions, the last a 19-yard TD pass to Kelvin Martin, which set the NCAA career passing record. Army cut BC's lead to a touchdown with 12:28 left, but the Eagles mixed runs and passes, finishing with a 13-yard TD to Martin.

GAME 8 STATS

Score	Comp.	Att.	Yds.	Pct.	Int.	TD passes	BC rush.	Flutie att./rush	Sacks /yds.	BC fumb.	Score at half
45-31	19	29	311	.655	0	3	156	4/6	1/-8	1	28-14

GAME 9: NO. 13 BC 24, SYRACUSE 16
November 17, Sullivan Stadium (60,890 Sellout), Regional TV

When word reached Foxborough that Navy was upsetting No. 2 South Carolina, the Big Three Jan. 1 bowls were suddenly very interested in BC—as long as it beat Syracuse. Though Flutie began by completing three passes into an 18-28 mph wind for a 7-0 lead, doubts grew when Syracuse kicked a field goal to end the first half ahead, 10-7. The Eagles suddenly stopped relying upon Flutie (only 3 of 6 for 27 yards in the second half) and started running 28 for 170 in the half). BC's defense was allowed to rest between series and held Syracuse to 110 yards on 41 rushes. Troy Stradford's 5-yard TD gave BC a 14-10 lead late in the third quarter, but he reinjured his hamstring and didn't return. On the next possession, Flutie ran a third-and-22 QB draw for 28 yards, setting up a Kevin Snow field goal. Kelvin Martin's 78-yard TD punt return down the left sideline apparently ensured the win, until Syracuse drove for a 36-second TD to close to within 8 (missed two-point conversion). The Orangemen regained the ball with less than two minutes left, but Tony Thurman's 10th interception of the year saved the game. "That ball had Jan. 1 written all over it," said Thurman, a prophet: 90 minutes after the game, BC unofficially accepted a bid to the Cotton Bowl.

GAME 9 STATS

Score	Comp.	Att.	Yds.	Pct.	Int.	TD passes	BC rush.	Flutie att./rush	Sacks /yds.	BC fumb.	Score at half
24-16	10	21	136	.476	1	0	270	11/81	1/-7	0	7-10

GAME 10: NO. 10 BC 47, NO. 12 MIAMI 45
November 23, Orange Bowl (30,235), National TV

The personalities of the two best quarterbacks in college football emerged and controlled one of the most exciting games ever. Flutie completed his first 11 passes into the rain and wind for a 14-0 lead, then watched Miami sophomore quarterback Bernie Kosar complete 11 straight for 14-14. Both excelled at what they did best: Flutie scrambled, throwing on the run, and Kosar threw pre-sack passes to his fourth receiver. When Miami drove for a touchdown and a 45-41 lead with 28 seconds left, Flutie nodded and took over at his 20. While Kosar celebrated on the sideline, Flutie hit 2 of 3, leaving him 6 seconds and 48 yards from a touchdown. Coaches tried to send in a messenger with the play, but Flutie sent him back; he wanted the players he had to run "55 Flood Tip." Four Eagles sprinted down the right sideline while Flutie scrambled from a three-man rush, planted and threw 65 yards to roommate Gerard Phelan, who with no time left stood unnoticed, the only player in the right side of the wet end zone, with the ball.

GAME 10 STATS

Score	Comp.	Att.	Yds.	Pct.	Int.	TD passes	BC rush.	Flutie att./rush	Sacks /yds.	BC fumb.	Score at half
47-45	34	46	472	.739	0	3	155	5/45	0/0	1	28-21

GAME 11: NO. 8 BC 45, HOLY CROSS 10
December 1, Fitton Field (25,000 Sellout), Local TV

Two first-half interceptions ruined Flutie's goal of the passing efficiency title, but he did throw his first touchdown pass to brother Darren and added a 39-yarder to Kelvin Martin. Troy Stradford broke the game open with a 44-yard TD run early in the third quarter, and BC's defense forced seven turnovers. Trivia: What was Flutie's final regular season play? A second-and-11 handoff to fullback Steve Strachan, who gained 5 yards to the BC 38. Flutie left with 12:40 remaining, and he and coach Jack Bicknell were carried off the field by teammates.

GAME 11 STATS

Score	Comp.	Att.	Yds.	Pct.	Int.	TD passes	BC rush.	Flutie att./rush	Sacks /yds.	BC fumb.	Score at half
45-10	13	25	276	.520	2	3	234	1/-13	1/13	1	17-10

1981

Opponent	Score	Comp. Att.	Pct.	Yds.	Int	TD	BC rush	BC fumb.	Score at half
*at Penn State	7-38	8-18	.444	135	1	1	94	4	0-24
NAVY	10-25	14-25	.550	118	1	0	118	2	10-16
at Army	41-6	15-21	.714	244	0	3	264	0	27-0
PITTSBURGH	24-29	23-42	.548	347	2	2	68	2	10-20
UMASS	52-22	13-25	.520	201	0	0	264	2	38-14
at Syracuse	17-27	11-22	.500	234	0	0	219	0	7-3
RUTGERS	27-21	9-22	.409	122	3	1	281	0	14-14
at Holy Cross	28-24	12-17	.706	251	1	2	108	2	14-14
TOTAL	206-190	105-192	.547	1652	8	10	1416	12	120-105

* entered game in fourth quarter

1982

Opponent	Score	Comp. Att.	Pct.	Yds.	Int	TD	BC rush	BC fumb.	Score at half
At Texas A&M	38-16	18-26	.692	356	1	3	120	0	24-6
at Clemson	17-17	18-35	.514	242	2	1	101	1	0-14
at Navy	31-0	19-36	.528	279	0	3	115	4	7-0
TEMPLE	17-7	18-36	.500	266	1	0	120	1	7-7
at W. Virginia	13-20	9-33	.273	122	4	0	141	2	3-6
RUTGERS	14-13	15-40	.375	239	1	1	249	1	0-10
at Army	32-17	11-27	.407	173	2	2	133	0	12-14
PENN STATE	17-52	26-44	.591	520	2	1	61	4	10-31
at UMass	34-21	11-28	.393	205	2	0	215	0	17-7
HOLY CROSS	35-10	10-20	.500	205	1	1	179	1	28-3
(TB) Auburn	26-33	22-38	.579	299	2	2	115	3	10-23
TOTAL	**284-219**	**184-386**	**.477**	**3048**	**22**	**15**	**1821**	**18**	**125-134**

(TB) = Tangerine Bowl, Orlando, Fla.

1983

Opponent	Score	Comp. Att.	Pct.	Yds.	Int	TD	BC rush	BC fumb.	Score at half
MORGAN ST.	45-12	15-27	.556	227	3	2	112	2	28-6
CLEMSON	31-16	20-36	.556	223	1	2	281	3	3-13
at Rutgers	42-22	6-8	.750	139	0	1	170	1	19-9
WEST VIRGINIA	17-27	23-51	.451	418	3	0	87	1	10-24
at Temple	18-15	17-28	.607	271	0	1	134	1	7-7
at Yale	42-7	18-26	.692	325	0	4	164	1	33-0
(s) PENN STATE	27-17	24-43	.558	380	1	2	113	3	24-10
at Army	34-14	15-29	.517	262	1	4	218	3	27-0
at Syracuse	10-21	12-36	.333	114	3	0	170	1	7-14
(s) HOLY CROSS	47-7	13-32	.406	177	2	0	385	1	10-0
(s) ALABAMA	20-13	14-29	.483	198	1	1	152	1	6-6
(LB) Notre Dame	18-19	17-36	.472	287	1	3	93	0	12-19
TOTAL	351-190	194-381	.509	3011	16	20	2110	18	186-89

(s) = game played at Sullivan Stadium

(LB) = Liberty Bowl, Memphis

1984

Opponent	Score	Comp. Att.	Pct.	Yds.	Int	TD	BC rush	BC fumb.	Score at half
W. CAROLINA	44-24	22-31	.710	330	1	4	258	0	34-7
at Alabama	38-31	19-38	.500	254	0	2	152	1	14-24
N. CAROLINA	52-20	28-38	.737	354	0	6	258	0	28-0
TEMPLE	24-10	17-33	.515	257	3	1	140	1	9-7
at W. Va.	20-21	21-42	.500	299	0	1	19	1	20-6
RUTGERS	35-23	21-30	.700	318	2	3	121	2	21-10
at Penn St.	30-37	29-53	.547	447	2	1	113	3	17-17
ARMY	45-31	19-29	.655	311	0	3	156	1	28-14
SYRACUSE	24-16	10-21	.476	136	1	0	270	0	7-10
at Miami	47-45	34-46	.739	472	0	3	155	1	28-21
at Holy Cross	45-10	13-25	.520	276	2	3	234	1	17-10
TOTAL	**404-268**	**233-386**	**.604**	**3454**	**11**	**27**	**1876**	**11**	**223-126**